Music and Mind in Everyday Life

Eric Clarke
Faculty of Music
University of Oxford

Nicola Dibben
Department of Music
University of Sheffield

Stephanie Pitts
Department of Music
University of Sheffield

OXFORD
UNIVERSITY PRESS

OXFORD

UNIVERSITY PRESS

Great Clarendon Street, Oxford ox2 6DP

Oxford University Press is a department of the University of Oxford.
It furthers the University's objective of excellence in research, scholarship,
and education by publishing worldwide in

Oxford   New York

Auckland   Cape Town   Dar es Salaam   Hong Kong   Karachi
Kuala Lumpur   Madrid   Melbourne   Mexico City   Nairobi
New Delhi   Shanghai   Taipei   Toronto

With offices in

Argentina   Austria   Brazil   Chile   Czech Republic   France   Greece
Guatemala   Hungary   Italy   Japan   Poland   Portugal   Singapore
South Korea   Switzerland   Thailand   Turkey   Ukraine   Vietnam

Oxford is a registered trade mark of Oxford University Press
in the UK and in certain other countries

Published in the United States
by Oxford University Press Inc., New York

© Eric Clarke, Nicola Dibben, Stephanie Pitts, 2010

The moral rights of the author have been asserted
Database right Oxford University Press (maker)

First published 2010

British Library Cataloguing in Publication Data

Data available

Library of Congress Cataloging in Publication Data

Data available

Typeset in Minion by Cepha Imaging Private Ltd., Bangalore, India
Printed in Great Britain
on acid-free paper by
Clays Ltd., St Ives plc

ISBN 978-0-19-852557-8

10 9 8 7 6 5 4 3 2 1

Contents

Chapter 1

Music in people's lives

1.1 The impact and ubiquity of music

Music pervades everyday life: in homes, on trains and planes, in cars and shops, at births and deaths, at weddings and at war, in concert halls, clubs, stadiums, and fields. In sporting events, at state occasions, in religious rituals, at the start of a new year, century or millennium, music marks and orchestrates the ways in which people experience the world together. What is it that makes people want to live their lives to the sound of music, and why do so many of our most private experiences and most public spectacles incorporate – or even depend upon – music?

To illustrate the approach taken in this book we start with an example that was widely experienced at the time, and is readily accessible through descriptions and online video. The funeral of Diana Spencer, Princess of Wales, took place on September 6, 1997 in Westminster Abbey in London, and was viewed by a worldwide audience estimated at 2 billion people. Music played a central role in the ceremony, and involved both the congregation present at the service and the wider audience watching and hearing the events in public places on screens and over public address systems, or watching and listening at home. A simple description of the music involved in the service is given in Section 1.1.1 and demonstrates the wide variety of musical genres that featured in the service: hymns, organ music, arrangements of concert music, a National Anthem, an Irish folk tune, contemporary art music, a pop ballad. A remarkable number of psychological processes and psychological functions associated with music are encapsulated within the 45 minutes occupied by the service.

Social conventions, developed over many centuries, have led to the specific ways in which music is incorporated into this or any other funeral, but this cultural development runs in parallel with the *psychological* functions that music can perform on such an occasion.

The psychological functions of this music for those who participated in, or witnessed, the event fall into four broad categories: (1) Ordering and organizing time; (2) Representing and expressing people and values; (3) Controlling and facilitating participation and observation; (4) Channelling and expressing emotions.

1.1.1 **Ordering and organizing time**

As the synopsis below demonstrates, the music has an important time-ordering role, with an alternation between 'performed' and

---

Synopsis of music at the funeral of Diana Spencer, Pricess of Wales

1. Organ music before the service, including music by Albinoni, J. S. Bach, Bridge, Dvořák, Elgar, Mendelssohn, Pachelbel, Parry, and Vaughan Williams.

2. The congregation sings 'God Save the Queen', the British National Anthem.

3. The funeral sentences sung by the Abbey choir to music by William Croft and Henry Purcell.

4. Hymn: 'I vow to thee, my country', with music by Gustav Holst.

5. Giuseppe Verdi: *Requiem* ('Libera me') sung by Lynne Dawson and the BBC singers.

6. Hymn: 'The King of love my shepherd is'.

7. Elton John's 'Goodbye England's Rose' (official song title, 'Candle in the Wind 1997', a version of his 1973 song 'Candle in the Wind').

8. Hymn: 'Make me a channel of your peace'.

9. *Air* from County Derry (commonly sung to the words 'Danny Boy'), sung by the Abbey choir (to the words 'I would be true' by Howard Arnold Walter).

10. Hymn: 'Guide me O thou great redeemer'.

11. Coffin leaves the Abbey to music by John Tavener (*Song for Athene*) with texts from *Hamlet* and the Greek Orthodox funeral service, sung by the choir.

collective music making. The solo organ music at the start provides a focus (but a significantly 'abstract' focus) for the members of the congregation as they assemble and wait for the arrival of the cortège and the beginning of the service itself. The music masks environmental sounds and in doing so it serves to demarcate the physical space as one which is different from the 'everyday', and provides aural privacy between waiting members of the congregation. Once the funeral cortège has entered the Abbey, the singing of the National Anthem by the whole congregation (as well as many others watching the service on huge screens in London and elsewhere) marks the start of the service proper, and serves to involve all those present in collective action. The remainder of the music (see synopsis above) both punctuates and structures the 45 minutes of the funeral service: at a practical and tangible level, it provides a pacing device for the transport of the coffin up to its position before the altar at the beginning of the service, during which the choir sings the funeral sentences; and then to the doors of the Abbey, while the choir sings John Tavener's *Song for Athene*. In terms of psychological pacing, it provides the congregation with opportunities for reflection and contemplation, such as during the singing of the *Air* from County Derry; interspersed with more arousing episodes, such as during the extract from the Verdi *Requiem*.

1.1.2 Representing people and expressing values

A funeral service is always, in some way, a representation of the individual who has died, and in the case of Diana, this important function was mixed in a complex fashion with her state persona. Music's lack of fixed and determinate meanings allows it to play a significant role in this representation, particularly in the context of the antagonisms, controversies, and conflicts that surrounded Diana's life and death. The organ music that preceded the service facilitated a period of calm reflection for the assembling congregation, and performed an important practical function in filling and 'sounding out' the time that was inevitably needed to assemble and organize the large number of people that attended. However, the musical choices represent Diana and her death in a range of more or less explicit ways: the music conforms to Western classical conventions of slow tempo and minor mode to represent and express mourning, and at the same time represents various aspects of Diana as a person, but in ways that are sufficiently abstract as to avoid controversy. 'Nimrod' from Elgar's *Enigma Variations* is often used as an expression of Englishness (and hence signifies Diana's own English aristocratic origins, as well as her position in relation to the British monarchy), while Vaughan Williams' *Prelude on the hymn tune Rhosymedre* (a Welsh hymn tune) represents another aspect of Diana's public persona – Princess of Wales. The use of music by J. S. Bach, a canonic composer of art music, confirms the high status that a state event of this kind suggests, while the inclusion of two of the most popular pieces of classical music (Pachelbel's *Canon* and the *Adagio* by Albinoni) represents Diana's own image as 'the people's princess'[1] and provides the familiarity that draws the congregation into the occasion.

The specific manner of the various performances also provides different representations and ways of engaging with the proceedings. The invisibility and anonymity of the two organists, hidden away up in the organ loft, who played prior to the service (and again after it) give the music a disembodied and 'de-personalized' quality – in the context of which individual members of the congregation can involve themselves in private thoughts. By contrast, Elton John's performance of 'Goodbye England's Rose' is highly personal, in the sense that both his physical presence as the performer (a centre of focus in the aisle of the Abbey and for the TV coverage that was broadcast around the world) and his status as the composer of the song make him the 'spotlit' performer of a tribute to Diana, with whom he had a well-known personal attachment. Elton John himself stands for the popular culture with which Diana was associated, and with the world of celebrity fashion of which both she and Elton John were or are representatives. And the original subject matter of the 1973 song ('Candle in the Wind'), of which 'Goodbye England's Rose' was a textual variant, was the life of Marilyn Monroe, another 'beautiful, tragic woman' who died at the same age as Diana and also

---

[1] 'The people's princess' was the phrase used by the then prime minister, Tony Blair, to describe Diana when he first responded to the news of her death on BBC television on August 31, 1997.

under controversial circumstances. In these and other ways, the song performs an important semiotic function in relation to Diana, and communicates Elton John's perspective on a range of much-discussed and controversial public attitudes to Diana, but in a manner that avoids the explicitness of verbal declarations.

Between the opposite poles of the performative anonymity of the organ playing on the one hand, and the pop-star performance of Elton John on the other, stand both the Abbey choir and the BBC singers with Lynne Dawson. The choir has something of the abstract character of the organ playing – de-personalized, and somewhat remote by virtue of the style and historical age of many of the texts and music that they sing. Like Elton John, however, Lynne Dawson is a visible and singular performer of the music and text that she sings – a 'mouthpiece' for its particular content. The music is, of course, not hers (in the way that it is for Elton John) but Verdi's, and the text is the standard Latin of the funeral mass. But to have a woman sing 'Libera me' – whose text deals with death, anger, calamity, and woe, as well as liberation from eternal death – at the funeral of a woman whose troubled and controversial private life had attracted huge media coverage provides a striking opportunity to express at one remove some of the conflicting thoughts and emotions that had been swirling around in the week after Diana's fatal car crash. In short, in the specific context of its performance, the music invites the congregation and wider audience to recognize parallels or identifications between the music with its conventional text and the life (real or imagined) of Diana, and in doing so, gives voice to people's emotions.

1.1.3 Controlling and facilitating participation and observation

As well as commemorating and representing Diana, the funeral service also provided an opportunity for people to participate in a collective action that expressed and embodied a certain kind of solidarity and shared experience – just as collective singing also does at political and sporting events, seasonal celebrations, and so on. The pattern of the funeral service provided an alternation of 'performed' and participatory music making, which allowed the congregation to both experience and reflect upon other people's representations of Diana, and also to be part of a collective manifestation. There are other ways in which such collective action might take place (co-ordinated speaking or dancing, for example), but music is particularly effective at co-ordinating large numbers of people, irrespective of age and physical fitness, in a social action that is highly structured and aesthetically rewarding.

1.1.4 Channelling and expressing emotions

The death of Diana elicited an unprecedented public response, and part of the function of the subsequent funeral (as with all funerals, of course) was to provide a focus and medium within which people, in the Abbey and all around the world, could express the strong emotions that they were experiencing. Music has long been recognized as a powerful means to elicit emotional responses, and as a channel for the sometimes unfocussed and unarticulated emotions that people may feel in the face of shocking or bewildering situations. Music can perform both arousing and cathartic functions, and both can be seen in the music used in Diana's funeral service. The National Anthem at the start of the service has an obviously ceremonial role, but after the generally gloomy, minor mode, slow music that preceded it, the major mode and more assertive rhythms of the anthem – sung by the whole congregation – can be seen as a way to instil a kind of emotional strength for the service that follows. Arguably, the primary function performed by all of the congregational music used in the service (see synopsis above) is to be emotionally supporting and rousing, since it uses rhythmic and tonal devices that are strongly associated in Western culture with positive and active emotions. The very act of singing, involving deliberately deep breathing, the increased muscle tone associated with standing up, and the concentration required to follow the words and music, also brings together physiological and psychological phenomena commonly used to help people to cope with, and overcome, strong negative emotions.

By contrast, the non-congregational music gives voice to the more negative emotions of grief and anger that characterized the publicly expressed reaction to Diana's death – providing a cathartic outlet for those emotions. A funeral service has to find a way to both recognize the grief, loss and perhaps anger that people inevitably feel at a death, and to encourage people to find consolation and some kind of hope. As it is difficult, for untrained singers in particular, to sing while in the grip of powerful negative emotions, it is also practical to give the more painful expressions of grief to the trained singers who have more highly developed vocal control, and more experience of singing in emotionally charged situations.

1.1.5 Performance processes

Having considered the functions and impact of the music at this funeral for the congregation and wider audience, it is also worth recognizing the complex psychological processes that are involved for the producers of that music. The service embraces a number of different kinds of performance, which depend on a range of psychological processes. There are the solo performances of the two organists who participated, involving sophisticated score reading skills, the complex and finely controlled co-ordination of hands and feet, and the skills of timing, voicing and articulation required to play the music expressively. There is Elton John's solo performance at the piano, involving musical and verbal memory skills (an old song with new words memorized in the few days before the service), the coordination of a looser vocal delivery with his own more anchored piano accompaniment, and the improvised embellishments in both the vocal and piano parts. And there are the highly organized, and rehearsed, ensemble performances of both the Abbey choir (involving young boys as well as men), and the BBC singers with their soloist Lynne Dawson. Finally there is the congregational singing of hymns and the National Anthem, involving a complex mixture of reading and recalling both words and music, and large-scale coordination between the choir, the congregation, and the organ.

1.1.6 The role of general psychological functions

As is perhaps already evident, the specific psychological processes that can be identified in the music at Diana's funeral depend upon more general psychological functions that underpin the human capacity for music, and for other psychological capacities beyond music. One of the attractions of studying music from a psychological perspective is the way in which such an approach engages with wider questions of human perception and action, emotion and cognition, development and expertise. Understanding how music can help to express or channel people's emotions, for instance, necessarily involves understanding a whole range of psychological capacities: how it is that people pick up and make sense of musical sounds, which in turn are part of the more general field of auditory perception; the relationship between words, sounds, and emotions; cathartic and stimulating functions in emotional life; the representation of emotions in different cultural contexts, and so on. In a similar manner, understanding the skills and psychological capacities required by a solo performance of the kind that Elton John gave at Diana's funeral might involve an understanding of general theories of memory and attention, of the nature and origins of expression in performance, and of the cognitive, psychodynamic, and social components of performance anxiety and its control – just as a study of the specific musical skills of the Abbey choirboys might need to engage with more general theories of human development and music education. Seen from one perspective, this is the strength of such an approach: it connects the study of relatively distinct musical phenomena with the much wider field of the human sciences (psychology, sociology, anthropology, neuroscience). However, it also raises significant challenges for the researcher who may need to acquire knowledge and expertise in a potentially bewildering range of disciplines.

1.2 Music and psychology

Broadly speaking, a psychological approach to music encompasses a range of empirical and theoretical research which seeks to understand music and its associated behaviour. The qualities which help to explain music's pervading presence in society also explain some of its interest as a domain for psychological study. First, music is temporal: a piece of music cannot be compressed, stretched, or reordered without changing its properties and sound – it takes place over time, and can happen concurrently with other activities and behaviour. Music becomes integrated with other aspects of society, acting as background music and creating ambience, as well as being presented in particular settings for concentrated listening. Second, the different kinds of musical activity – playing, composing, and listening to music – allow varied types and levels of involvement and skill. Many of these provide rich domains in which to study generic aspects of psychological functioning. Musical performance, for example, involves complex motor skills, allowing investigation of the planning and execution of movements, of memory, and of skill acquisition. Third, music is made and experienced by groups of widely varying sizes as well as individuals, allowing investigation of processes of entrainment, interaction, and communication. Lastly, music is a widespread human activity: there is no society which does not have music, and for many people, music is both significant and life-enhancing. For these different reasons, the study of music from a psychological perspective is a rich domain for understanding human behaviour and thought.

Over the last 150 years, the 'psychology of music', sometimes called 'music psychology', has acquired the status of a distinct research domain, heavily influenced by contemporary academic psychology. The psychology of music differs from musicology, which tends to be concerned with the history and analysis of musical texts, and also from the sociology of music, which focuses on the social and political contexts and functions of musical activities. It includes cognitive research, focusing for example on perception memory, motor skills, and emotional responses; investigations of musical development, such as how musical skills and enthusiasms are acquired and nurtured; and social psychological questions of musical taste, interaction and communication. In the contemporary academic context, it takes its place alongside empirical musicology, systematic musicology and cognitive ethnomusicology[2] in offering a broadly analytical perspective on musical understanding and experience.

---

[2] For a range of disciplinary perspectives on empirical research in music, see *Empirical Musicology* (Clarke and Cook, 2004) and the online journal *Empirical Musicology Review*. For an introduction to cognitive musicology see Pirkko Moisala (1995), and for definitions

Thus the psychology of music, with its origins in scientific and experimental approaches, brings together a variety of theoretical approaches and empirical methods. These empirical methods involve gathering information by systematically observing musical behaviour, undertaking experiments designed to isolate particular aspects of musical understanding and action, or administering questionnaires and carrying out interviews. While some studies are exploratory and others test hypotheses, most use the inductive reasoning favoured in the physical sciences, making a set of observations and drawing a general principle from those findings. In this sense, the psychology of music is descriptive rather than prescriptive: it identifies robust patterns or principles that help to explain behaviour in the world but, like any other science, does not claim to provide ultimate 'proofs'. To the extent that these theories or explanations help to inform and predict behaviour, the psychology of music is also instrumentalist, with relevance to contexts beyond the specific experimental situation, and the potential for practical applications.

Research in the psychology of music can seem at times to be somewhat removed from the reality of musical experience, isolating as it does particular phenomena for systematic investigation. An experiment designed to measure the emotional responses of listeners, for example, may involve participants in listening under artificial conditions rather than in the concert hall, since data gathered in the 'real world' context would be affected by uncontrollable factors such as the presence of other listeners, the temperature, lighting and acoustics in the hall, and the physical distance of the listener from the performers. By controlling each of these variables in an experimental setting, researchers are able to generate data that are easier to interpret and that produce robust findings, since the range of likely explanations for the results has been reduced. In addition, the experiment can be replicated and its findings tested against other results with different listeners or different kinds of music: they are generalizable beyond the specific

---

of cognitive ethnomusicology and links to current research, see http://ethnomusicology. osu.edu/EMW/CEMprogrdes.html. A discussion of systematic musicology is provided by Marc Leman and Albrecht Schneider (1997).

instance of one concert-hall setting. The findings are still relevant to real world listening, but the distractions of being in a live audience are acknowledged in the interpretation rather than the design of the experiment. By emphasizing experimental control over musical realism as in this example, the psychology of music has taken a particular route towards understanding musical behaviour. An investigation of the experience of being in a real audience forms a rather different kind of study – and one which, until very recently, has tended not to be the focus of research in psychology of music.

1.3 **What a psychological approach can and cannot do**

Psychology has an important role in developing an understanding of musical behaviour and experience, and in doing so sheds light on mental and social processes more widely. However, it is important to acknowledge the limitations of this approach, and in particular, to recognize that music psychology cannot necessarily generate practical answers or 'recipes for success' in musical endeavours. In investigating strategies for practising a musical instrument, for example, research in the psychology of music has useful things to say on a number of topics: what might be the most effective length and focus for regular practice sessions; whether or not to do slow practice; what kind of family support seems to foster children's motivation to learn; what strategies are effective in giving children confidence in performing; or what impact the influence of peers, siblings, parents, and teachers has upon musical development. These findings might seem to offer some directly applicable 'solutions' for those involved in supporting the acquisition of musical skill, but this is true to only a limited extent. Research into the psychology of musical performance reveals the complexity of influences on musical skill development, and is therefore not readily translated into a generally applicable set of principles or solutions. The idea that music psychology will provide a formula for producing better players more easily is simplistic. A more realistic aim is for research in music psychology to reveal reliable or systematic patterns of behaviour, including those associated with success in musical performance – however that may be defined.

The psychology of music has contributions to make in fostering interdisciplinary perspectives and furthering understanding of musical and psychological phenomena outside its own boundaries. Indeed, thinking in terms of 'subjects of study' rather than in terms of 'disciplines' highlights the continuity between psychological and other approaches. In forging links with music theory and analysis, for instance, music psychology can offer an empirical perspective on theoretical accounts of musical understanding, revealing whether and how specific aspects of musical organisation are experienced – whether they have 'psychological reality'. Far from undermining music theory, as might be suspected, the psychology of music can highlight the culturally creative role of theory and analysis, offering an investigative approach to how analyses are understood and used in musical learning and experience, and how they contribute to musical culture and discourse.

Empirical methods also offer a means to attempt a reconstruction of aspects of past musical experience and practices. For example, quantifying the occurrence of pitch classes in Gregorian chant provides a measure of the perceived hierarchical importance of pitches within modes, which may or may not agree with their designated modal identity, and which has been used as the basis of one possible (if contentious) account of the emergence of the major or minor system in the 17th century.[3] In another example, psychoacoustic principles have been used to provide an explanation for the rules of voice leading in Western music of the common practice era: practices of polyphonic writing, such as the avoidance of consecutive perfect fifths, and the maintenance of a larger interval between bass line and upper voices than between the upper voices, avoid tonal fusion and promote the perception of individual voices.[4] As these examples illustrate, a psychological approach can both complement historical musicology and provide possible underlying explanations for common musical practices.

---

[3] See David Huron and Joshua Veltman (2006); the same issue of the journal includes a critique of this approach by Frans Wiering.

[4] For further explanation, see David Huron (2001).

Many studies within music psychology explore the influence of enculturation on musical experiences and of how material and cultural conditions are reflected in musical sound and practices. From this perspective, psychological approaches can contribute to ethnomusicological study by offering methods for the systematic investigation of musical behaviours and thinking. For example, methods developed in music psychology offer possible ways to study musical experiences without relying on language or introspection, and so can be helpful in distinguishing between people's demonstrable cognitive strategies and their articulated perceptions of their own behaviour.

Beyond musicology, music provides a fascinating range of phenomena within which to explore generic psychological capacities, and is therefore a rewarding domain for psychologists interested in memorization, motor skills, perception and learning, enculturation, and affect. Piano performance, for example, offers an ideal context in which to study the timing and spatial control of finger and arm movements, hand–eye coordination, and so on. A comparable domain is the study of touch-typists, but the variety of movements, overall complexity of the actions and planning, and the range of skill levels of pianists offers a far greater range of possibilities for researchers.

1.4 What this book is about

Musical behaviour can be broadly understood as comprising three elements: making music, using music, and acquiring music. In this book, we address each of these in turn, considering the real world experience of encountering music in each of these ways and evaluating what the psychology of music says or could say about them. The primary focus is on understanding musical behaviour, by relating academic knowledge to concrete musical situations and experiences. As in this chapter, we present actual and fictionalized accounts of musical experiences, in order to embed research in realistic contexts. By drawing together existing research, the book reveals what a psychological approach can do and why it is important to anyone wanting to understand musical experience. As well as considering the potential of the psychological study of musical behaviour, it also highlights some of its problems and limitations.

The purpose of the book is not to represent music psychology simply as it is, but rather to examine how a psychological approach can shed light on a range of musical phenomena – and that means considering new research that could be undertaken in this field, as well as what already exists. The balance of topics in this book therefore does not reflect the dominance of various topics in the psychology of music as it currently stands: for example, the huge amount of attention given to the perception and cognition of music is dealt with relatively succinctly here, whereas we devote substantial space to thinking through the implications of a psychological approach for understanding how music is used, despite a comparative scarcity of existing research on that topic. Similarly, although examples drawn from the published literature reflect its focus on Western art music, we provide other examples where possible and suggest ways in which research findings from one genre may be relevant (or not) to other musics. The advantage of this approach is that it privileges what the psychology of music has to say about musical experience in real contexts.

This book is aimed at anyone interested in discovering more about the psychological basis of musical experiences. It is intended to show what kinds of questions about music can be tackled using a psychological approach, which methods are used to do this, and how a psychological approach is, or might be, relevant to other areas of musicology or allied disciplines.

Part 1

Making music

At some point in their lives, almost everyone makes music – whether in the informal context of singing 'Happy Birthday' for a relative, or in the more obvious activities of playing in an orchestra or writing a song for a friend. Music is made under the most diverse kinds of circumstances and by all kinds of people, of whom only a few would describe themselves as musicians. For a few people, music making will be the primary focus of their lives, although the way in which the term 'making music' is understood in different cultural contexts is extremely variable. In the Western classical tradition, a rather sharp distinction is made between the compositional aspect of 'making' music and the performance aspect of 'making' music, with various kinds of improvisation occupying some sort of middle ground. But in many other traditions, the distinction seems much less clear or much less relevant (think of singer-songwriters, for example), as it is also for the huge variety of ways in which people make music informally as part of their everyday lives (humming at the bus stop, singing at a football match, singing along with the radio while getting ready to go to school).

The aim of this section is to explore the psychological processes involved in making music in all its various manifestations, and to consider what light has been shed on those processes by psychological research. What are the motivations that lead people to make music at all? What general psychological skills and capacities are required to make music? How is musical performance communicative and expressive? What is involved in making music through improvisation and composition? We start with a discussion of what drives people to make music at all, and the kinds of skills that music makers demonstrate.

Chapter 2

Motivations and skills

2.1 Motivations

Since music-making is so ubiquitous in human cultures but does not obviously seem to play a role in human survival, why is it that virtually everyone seems to do it? What motivates people to make music? There are various broadly sociological or cultural approaches to this question, which draw upon the particular values that music-making demonstrates in different cultural contexts, including demonstrations of 'cultural capital', religious functions, the establishment and maintenance of social integration and particular cultural allegiances, self-expression, and so on. But from a developmental perspective, strong claims have also been made about the close association between the fundamental communicative needs of human infants and the development of musical competence. In simple terms, the idea is that the development of music-making skills is inextricably bound up with an infant's exploration and discovery of communicative interaction.

Human infants are almost completely dependent upon their adult caregivers, and are born with very powerful yet relatively undifferentiated and 'unformed' perceptual and motor skills. The developmental advantage of this is that it allows for enormous flexibility in infants' adaptations to their environments, but it also means that effective interaction between infants and their immediate human context is at a premium. If a newborn infant is to survive, it has to establish a powerful communicative and emotionally–invested relationship with its primary caregiver (usually its mother) at a stage in its development when it still has no language capacity and relatively unsophisticated sensorimotor skills. Vocalization, eye contact, and physical intimacy are the primary means by which the characteristically powerful bond between mother and infant is usually established. Over the first year of life, vocalization becomes an increasingly significant component of this developing relationship, leading towards the establishment of early infant language at around the age of 18 months or two years.

Infants' vocalizations during this prelinguistic period become increasingly structured, with progressive control over pitch, timing, and articulation. This 'babbling' has a very obviously protolinguistic character, but equally it has a protomusical character – as has been widely observed in developmental research. Colwyn Trevarthen[1], for example, has argued that extremely early infant–caregiver interaction has a specifically musical character, primarily by virtue of its rhythmically coordinated quality. Informal observation is consistent with this view: infants often seem to interact with their caregivers in what seems to be a coordinated and 'turn-taking' fashion, quite apart from the obvious singing quality of the babbling that emerges later on. But a different view might be to recognize that infants develop highly significant skills of motor, vocal, and timing control starting right from birth, and that these form the basis for a whole lot of subsequent skills and capacities – music and language among them.

Whatever the relative priority of music and language in this developmental process, it is certainly the case that parents and caregivers adopt a style of vocal interaction with their infants, widely referred to as *motherese*[2] or infant-directed speech, that is found in a wide range of human cultures and features particularly 'music-like' attributes. It tends to be higher in pitch than adult-to-adult speech, has more pronounced pitch contours, is slower, more temporally regular, and more repetitive; it also includes a greater proportion of clearly stressed elements. In short, it is melodious, and it has been shown that babies spend more time attending and responding to it than to non-infant-directed speech. It is worth noting that although infant-directed speech can give the impression that

----

[1] Colwyn Trevarthen makes the case for this fundamental attribute of music in Trevarthen (1999–2000). For further research on very early communication between infants and carers, see Trehub et al. (1997); Trehub and Trainor (1998); and the chapters by Hanus Papousek, Christoph Fassbender, Mechthild Papousek, and Viviane Pouthas in Deliège and Sloboda (1996).

[2] See, for example, Falk (2004).

the adult is trying to imitate the sounds of the infant, it is in fact the infant who imitates the adult: parents start talking to their infants this way long before they have heard the infant make such sounds.

Infant babbling, which starts at around 6–8 months, is very similar across a broad range of human cultures[3] and consists of repeated consonant–vowel pairs ('ma-ma', 'ga-ga', 'da-da-da') with a strong rhythmic quality and pitched character. This babbling allows the infant to experiment with and explore vocal control (which, by the time the young child is speaking and singing, will require the coordination of around 70 muscle systems), and also constitutes the basis for an obviously musical kind of behaviour. Infants and young children soon start to enjoy various kinds of vocal (as well as gestural) imitation games with their caregivers and other adults, and the ensuing vocal games are an important way in which developing skills are engaged to form a significant building block for emerging socialization as well as cognitive development. Playing – the word that is most commonly used for making music – has for a long time been recognized as a vital factor in human development.

One reason, therefore, why people seem to be almost universally motivated to make music at some point in their lives is that this playful, protomusical behaviour, which soon becomes more explicit in imitative songs, has a significant developmental role. The skills and capacities learned during this period of development occupy a fundamental position in a person's behaviour and psyche, with the result that almost everyone retains both an inclination *towards* making music and, paradoxically, a marked sensitivity to or awkwardness about public music-making (and singing in particular), perhaps because of the very deeply rooted functions that the singing and/or speaking voice plays in everyone's life.

The general pattern of human development provides a possible explanation for why music-making is so widespread, but clearly there is more to understanding what motivates people to make music than raw biology. Making music can be intrinsically rewarding for a number of

---

[3] See work by Barbara Davis and Peter MacNeilage (2000), and Peter Jusczyk (1997).

broadly psychological reasons: as we explore in more depth later in the book (see Part 2: Using music), music provides strong emotional experiences to which people are drawn; it facilitates a variety of positive social interactions (group membership, collaborative activity, social cooperation); it can play an important role in the construction and maintenance of identity, a matter to which we return at a number of places in this book; and it is an example of a complex skill, the acquisition and 'realization' of which can contribute to a person's sense of self-esteem. In more general social terms, music occupies a contradictory position as far as its cultural value is concerned: on the one hand, it is regarded as a dispensable 'luxury' or even a threat to social control (as demonstrated by attitudes to music in classical Greece, by the Taliban regime in Afghanistan, or in journalistic writing on jazz, rap, or heavy metal), and on the other hand, it is given an elevated status that invests it with significant 'cultural capital'.[4] In many cultures, musicians are given a privileged status, with the consequence that they become cultural icons or role models, and musical skills become 'assets' that children are encouraged to acquire by their parents or teachers.[5]

In summary, the motivations for most people to make music in one way or another emerge from a combination of developmental and social factors. The basic sensorimotor skills that infants need to develop for a whole range of human behaviours (the control of timing, vocalization, and movement) are vital to general human development, and are also fundamental components of music making. The actualization and development of those skills in a specifically musical context then provide intrinsic rewards through emotional engagement, social facilitation, identity formation, the exercise of 'mastery', and increased self-esteem. And in terms of the wider social context, although there are some circumstances in which music-making is actively discouraged, there are many more (both mainstream and countercultural) in which

---

[4] The idea that cultural activities or attributes can be understood as having more or less value, and that people will 'trade' on that value (summed up in the phrase 'cultural capital'), was developed by the French sociologist Pierre Bourdieu (1984).

[5] Antonia Ivaldi and Susan O'Neill (2008) have studied adolescents' musical role models.

music-making is invested with considerable cultural importance, and is thus regarded as a socially attractive or advantageous attribute.[6]

2.2 Skills in making music

The skills that are involved in playing music include the physical skills of instrumental or vocal performance, the perceptual and motor skills of coordinating with other performers, the expressive skills of playing music in a convincing or persuasive manner, and the social skills of knowing how to behave and feel comfortable in various performing situations (a religious occasion, a concert, the celebration of an event, or a performance exam). Consider the following specific example:

> Tim is a guitarist, sometimes doubling up on keyboard, in a four-piece pop band that gets most of its work playing at functions such as parties and weddings. Given the kind of work on which they depend, they've built up a large and eclectic repertoire ranging from 50s rock 'n' roll through glam rock and disco to a selection of 1990s 'favourites'. They seldom need to play more than about 20 numbers at any one event, but their total repertoire at any one time consists of well over 60 titles.

What are the skills that Tim has had to acquire to play music in this way, and how might they be understood from a psychological perspective? First, there are the motor skills involved in playing the guitar and keyboard, which are primarily concerned with the control of space, time, force, and coordination in movement. Skilled musicians in traditions ranging from Indonesian gamelan, Irish fiddle playing, Indian sitar, and Ghanaian drumming to Chinese opera, Japanese thrash metal bands, and European string quartets may have to produce

---

[6] In a number of publications (e.g. Cross, 2003), Ian Cross has discussed the relationship between biological and cultural factors in the significance of music.

in the region of 10 discrete movements per second in complex patterns involving the coordination of two or more limbs and with a spatial precision of less than a millimetre. How is this achieved? Since the beginning of the twentieth century, psychologists have been interested in trying to understand how motor skills are acquired and maintained, with a particular focus on the ways in which mental processes and the *intention* to make specific movements interact with the mechanical constraints of the human body. Influenced by the model of the computer and its distinction between hardware and software, a dominant approach since the 1970s has been the theory of 'motor programming'. The idea is that complex and rapid movements need to be planned in advance, since human reaction times are too long for one action to follow another in a simple linear chain, and that the mind or brain therefore has to put together a set of 'instructions' (similar to a computer program) that tells the various muscle systems what to do and when. Henry Shaffer and Caroline Palmer, among others, have studied motor programming in piano performance, using as evidence the errors that players make when the programming goes wrong, for instance, to theorize about how an otherwise invisible motor program might be organized.[7] If Tim (see above) can play the same material on either guitar or keyboard – which obviously involves completely different physical movements – his conception of what he wants to play must be more abstract than a simple set of movement instructions: it must be a kind of 'intention', presumably corresponding quite closely to some type of representation of the music, that is converted into specific actions only in the context of a particular instrument at his fingertips.

One criticism of the motor programming approach is that it treats the body simply as a passive mechanism to be pushed around by a central controller in whatever way the program dictates. This does not really reflect how skilled musicians *feel* they are using their bodies. It is certainly true that playing music can be physically frustrating, uncomfortable,

---

[7] See, for example, Shaffer (1981), Palmer (1989), and Palmer and van de Sande (1993). At an even more detailed level, studies have looked at the ways in which pianists organize their fingering patterns in performance (e.g. Sloboda et al., 1998; Parncutt et al., 1997).

and hard work: it *can* feel like an unwilling body trying to carry out impossible manoeuvres on an awkwardly organized instrument, driven by an unrealistic intention. But when expert players are in control of what they are doing, even when it is complex and challenging, the physical experience of playing can be rewarding and exhilarating. Mind, body, and instrument all seem to join up seamlessly, rather than feeling like three separate components at odds with one another. A rather different way to look at the musician's physical relationship with his or her instrument is therefore to consider the ways in which the design of the instrument, inherent characteristics of the body, and demands (or opportunities) of the music work together in an optimizing manner. The ethnomusicologist John Baily has pointed out the complex relationship between musical traditions, developments in instrument design, and the ergonomics of performance in Afghan music, where a new instrument affording new possibilities was developed, and gave rise to changes in the musical tradition itself that capitalized on the opportunities of the new instrument.[8] In musical traditions that use notation, such as Western classical music, performers have to find ways to *make* their bodies and instruments accomplish what the written music requires – hence the long hours of technical practice that expert performers have to put in. But in improvising traditions, there is a more fluid and dynamic relationship between the performers' capacities and the musical material. Players may choose in some cases to take the line of least resistance and produce what is either habitual or physically easy to manage and at other times to push the boundaries of both the musical material and their own physical control. Tim can either play a rather well-worn and undemanding solo in the middle of a cover version of Eric Clapton's 'Layla', particularly if no-one seems to be paying much attention, or have a go at something more risky and demanding, for example if there is someone in the audience who he is trying to impress.

---

[8] See John Baily's (1985) chapter on musical structure and human movement. In a slightly different manner, David Sudnow (2001) has discussed his own development as a jazz pianist, writing in a vivid manner about the changing relationship between his improvising intentions and the feeling of his hands at the piano.

Quite apart from getting around his guitar and keyboard, Tim also has to recall and keep track of the song that he is playing, coordinate with other members of the band, and try to cover up the inevitable gaps and errors that are bound to intrude in any live performance; in other words, he needs to be in control of a range of perceptual and cognitive skills. In two 35-minute sets, it is likely that he will have played in the region of 10 000 individual notes, which appears to be a prodigious feat of musical memory. How do musicians remember and control such large amounts of information? There is a large literature in the psychology of memory offering different explanations of how this vital human capacity might best be understood, but virtually all accounts agree that the capacity and persistence of memory primarily depends upon how information is organized. Unlike computers, human beings are very poor at remembering random data, and Tim's ability to remember the 10 000 notes that he needs for a night's work is a direct consequence of his ability to make use of redundancies and regularities in the material itself. In fact, because the music involves a significant amount of improvisation, the 10 000 notes that he plays are generated from a relatively sparse and schematic representation of each song: he does not have to actually *remember* anything like that amount. But Tim has a background in classical music, and in the final recital he gave for his music degree, he played Beethoven's *Hammerklavier* piano sonata from memory. On that occasion he really did have to produce more than 20 000 'right' notes from memory, in the right order! Research on memory in general, as well as more specifically on memory for music, shows that expert memorizers capitalize on regularities in the material to be remembered, which they either discover spontaneously or impose upon it. The conductor Toscanini appears to have had an extraordinary memory for music, on one occasion writing out all the individual parts for a string piece that he had decided that he wanted the orchestra to play at short notice, but for which the parts were not available – and which he had apparently not seen for decades.[9]

---

[9] This and other fascinating accounts of Toscanini's memory can be found in the chapter entitled 'Toscanini's memory' in a book on memory in everyday life edited by Ulric Neisser (1982). General reviews of theories of musical memory can be found in

In improvising traditions, as already noted, an important cognitive skill concerns the relationship between memory and invention. Being familiar with the various idioms that his band plays, Tim really only has to remember the outline structure for any song and its specific melodic materials, and can rely on his powers of invention to create the appropriate rhythms and chords in the course of performance, as well as improvised solos when these are required. This is similar to the way in which a storyteller might remember the main narrative outline of a story – the gist of it, in other words – and find or 'invent' the specific language in the act of telling, while making sure that only the important turns of phrase, such as a punch line or a joke based on a pun, are remembered literally. In the psychology of memory, the relationship between the more schematic and generalizable character of memory and its more literal counterpart is captured in the distinction between semantic and episodic memory. Semantic memory is generic (e.g. tonal and metric structures) and takes a specific form only in particular circumstances, whereas episodic memory is concerned with the encoding and retrieval of particular events. For an experienced guitarist, playing a blues in E minor is largely a matter of semantic memory supplemented by a degree of more or less formulaic 'invention', whereas playing Led Zeppelin's 'Stairway to Heaven' requires episodic memory for the particular chord sequence, rhythm, and melody.

Outside her working life (music does not earn her any money), Janice is an aspiring songwriter and plays the violin in a five-piece free improvisation ensemble called Cataract. Cataract are doing one of their occasional gigs in a local community centre, and are four minutes into their third number of the night. It has been going

Bob Snyder's (2000) book on music and memory, Robert Crowder's (1993) chapter on auditory memory, Aaron Williamon's (2002) chapter on memorizing music, Jane Ginsborg's (2004) chapter on different strategies for memorizing music, and chapter 6 of the Andreas Lehmann et al. (2007) book *Psychology for Musicians*. Roger Chaffin et al. (2002) provide an engaging and multifaceted account of piano performance and memory in their book *Practicing Perfection: Memory and Piano Performance*.

well – although Janice feels that they have been 'playing safe' and that there is a danger of predictability and tweeness. While she adds a bit of scurrying texture to her co-performer Rhodri's slow-moving tuba line, she picks up on three notes that sound to her (weirdly) like the beginning of the British National Anthem – and goes with them, suddenly breaking out of the contained texture with a distorting wildness that, even as she does it, reminds her of The Sex Pistols' famous deconstruction of the national anthem in 'God Save the Queen'. Using all the violent noisiness of the violin that she can muster, she rips up the anthem in what she notices, as her co-performers fall silent, becomes an extended solo of a minute or two, finishing with a dramatic down-bow (and a fair amount of broken bow hair) to enthusiastic applause.

Making music has so far in this chapter been understood mainly as playing music – but people also make music in the more obvious sense of 'making up' music. As we noted in the introduction to this section of the book, some cultures make a rather sharp distinction between composition, improvisation, and performance (contemporary European culture is one) whereas others do not (e.g. the song tradition of the Venda, as documented by John Blacking). Janice (above) 'makes music' in what she regards as two rather different ways: she improvises on the violin and she writes (composes) songs mostly on her own, at home, at the piano. Chapter 4 discusses improvisation and composition at greater length, but for now it is worth noting some of the particular skills that are involved in Janice's activities. Janice's Cataract performance depends on a very close interaction between listening and playing, which requires (among other things) what psychologists call selective attention.[10] Her distorted version of 'God Save the Queen'

---

[10] Discussions of selective attention – which often allude to what is called 'the cocktail party phenomenon' (attending to what someone is saying in a crowded and noisy room) – can be found in most standard texts on cognitive psychology, such as Eysenck and Keane (2005). A very influential approach to this whole issue, dealing specifically with speech and music, is Albert Bregman's (1990) landmark book *Auditory Scene Analysis*.

depends first on noticing those three tuba notes in the midst of the other simultaneous sounds, then attending to the sound of her own playing to make sure that she plays a pattern of notes that is (at least initially) sufficiently recognizable as the anthem, and at the same time noticing that her co-performers are falling silent one by one (she does this by ear since she often plays with her eyes shut). Another of Janice's skills is what might be called 'ear–hand' coordination: the ability to find on her violin a sound that she may have in her head, or, conversely, to recognize and make sense of the sounds that her body seems to be making on the instrument. At the same time, she needs to have the musical and social awareness that help her to gauge when to hold back, when to break out, when to make a contribution, and when to keep her silence.

Her songwriting depends on some of the same ear–hand skills (and ear–eye–hand skills, because she notates the words and music of her songs) as does her improvising, but it also depends on more sustained and slower-moving musical thinking. Because her songwriting style is fairly conventional, she works hard at the overall shape and coherence of the song and at achieving what she hopes is her own compositional 'voice'. This in turn depends on understanding the conventions of songwriting, how to achieve the effects that she likes in other people's songs, and so on. In other words, it depends crucially on having either intuitive or explicit understanding of musical structure, and the affordances of musical materials.[11] More than that, of course, it also depends on having what might be called the generative skill (and this is true of her improvising too) to know how to develop something that she has come across, such as a chord sequence, a rhythmic figure or a texture, in an interesting and novel manner.[12]

---

[11] The term *affordance* was coined by the psychologist James Gibson (see Gibson, 1966) to mean the opportunities for action that perceivers detect in the environment around them. We return to this idea in Chapter 5.

[12] The idea of generative skills has also been extensively used in accounts of ordinary language use (which has obviously 'compositional' and 'improvisational' components) and a whole variety of other human behaviours. We come back to these and related questions in the longer discussion of improvisation and composition in Chapter 4.

Just as structure plays a major part in understanding composition, improvisation, and musical memory, so too has it been invoked as a primary explanatory principle in understanding another important cognitive skill in playing music: playing from notation. Musicians with equal expertise as performers may differ dramatically in their sight-reading skills, and one way to explain this is in terms of their ability to see and make use of structure in the music – although there may also be more basic sensorimotor differences, such as visual scanning abilities and motor fluency. There is still a lot more to discover about the strategies or particular aptitudes of expert sight readers, but a good deal of the existing research has suggested that they may be able to make particularly effective use of the structure in musical notation, allowing them to look ahead more effectively. This more structured reading also provides them with a useful framework within which to improvise, or guess, if the demands of the notation become momentarily overwhelming, or if they have a lapse of concentration. Informed guessing is arguably the key to the success of a good sight-reading accompanist or repetiteur: it may often be impossible to keep track of all the details of a score, but a lot can be achieved (or got away with) if a player can keep going with more or less improvised material based on contextually appropriate pitches and rhythms, while finding their way back at the earliest opportunity to what is actually on the page. Research in other domains of cognitive expertise has also demonstrated the importance of structural awareness in achieving high levels of performance. A classic demonstration is Chase and Simon's study of chess players, in which they showed that expert players could remember the arrangement of the pieces on a chess board much better than novice players, but only if the arrangement conformed to a pattern that is actually 'legal' in chess (i.e. a legitimately structured arrangement); if pieces were simply randomly arranged on the board, experts were no better at remembering them than novices.[13]

---

[13] The study, which has become something of a classic in cognitive psychology, is discussed in Chase and Simon (1973). For some of the work on sight-reading, see Sloboda (1982), Waters et al. (1998), Lehmann and McArthur (2002), and Chapter 6 in Lehmann et al. (2007).

While chess and music-making may require similar cognitive skills, they require quite different social skills, and the social skills required by music-making differ from one performance context to another. At one extreme, some solitary and even reclusive individuals seem to be dedicated to the particular environment of the recording studio (Glenn Gould, or Brian Wilson from The Beach Boys might be examples), whereas at the other extreme, 'star' performers such as Madonna or the violinist Maxim Vengerov seem to thrive on the maximum possible public exposure. The social skills involved in these contexts may be rather different, but in every case musicians have to find ways to negotiate their interactions with other people: fellow musicians, producers, audience, worshippers, dancers, or examiners. These social interactions are tightly regulated under some circumstances (think of the specific etiquette that applies to the behaviour of a rock star at a stadium gig, an organist at a wedding, or a folk musician at a regular evening session[14]) and more informal at other times. But for all performing musicians, an unavoidable social skill that has to be acquired in one way or another is the ability to present themselves in public – to find a way to feel comfortable with their identity, persona, and musical competence in the face of public attention. There are many components to this aspect of a musician's identity, but one that looms large in the lives of many musicians in the Western tradition is how to cope with performance anxiety.

The great majority of classical performers appear to suffer from stage fright to a more or less debilitating extent, as well as a sizeable proportion of performers in other musical traditions; as a result, extensive research has been undertaken with the aim of understanding its origins, and finding ways to combat it or alleviate its effects via a range of coping strategies.[15] Stage fright is not only a significant practical problem for many musicians but also a palpable demonstration of the

---

14 Jonathan Stock (2004) has provided an account of such folk interactions.

15 See, for example, Elizabeth Valentine's (2002) chapter 'The fear of performance', 'Managing performance anxiety' in Lehmann et al. (2007), and Glenn Wilson's (1997) chapter 'Performance anxiety' – all of which provide informative summaries of research, theorizing, and practical advice in this area.

intensity with which social pressures bear down on performers, and the powerful feelings of vulnerability and fear of identity exposure that many musicians feel. Although performance anxiety may represent a particular pathology experienced in a specific type of musical culture exemplified by the Western classical concert culture, in more general terms it also exposes the power of the social forces at work in performance situations, and suggests the kinds of social skills that performers need to acquire just to survive in the music profession.

Summary

Making music requires the acquisition and coordination of a considerable range of skills: skills of motor control, coordination, and timing; reading skills in the case of notated musical traditions; skills of memorization; creative skills for composition and improvisation; and the social skills that making music with other people, and in front of other people, demands. Many of these specifically musical attributes overlap with, and probably depend on, psychological capacities of a much more general kind that underlie a whole range of other human activities such as speaking, playing games, engaging in social interactions, dancing, and acting. It is important to recognize the complex ways in which psychological explanations must necessarily interact with sociological and 'material culture' accounts – a matter to which we return at the end of Chapter 4. Janice's improvising, for example, has to be understood as the meeting point of her own psychological skills and processes, the social context in which she plays and the expectations and values that the context encapsulates, and what might be thought of as the accumulated history of the musical material with which she works. Her distorted take on the national anthem results from psychological processes (the technical skills of violin playing, musical memory, and the skill of attending selectively), sociological factors relating to the culture of contemporary European free improvisation (e.g. the acceptance and positive valorization of anti-establishment displays), and the values that are materially encapsulated in the British National

Anthem and its history – as well as the cultural history of The Sex Pistols, and perhaps punk and protest more generally, to which her own performance obliquely refers. An adequate account of an event of this kind necessarily involves a complex and cross-disciplinary web of explanations.[16]

---

16 Georgina Born's (2005) paper 'On musical mediation: ontology, technology and creativity' is one such attempt.

Chapter 3

Expression and communication in performance

3.1 **Expression**

A fundamental feature of almost every kind of music is the relationship between players and their material. Only in the extremes of free improvisation on the one hand and entirely studio-based music on the other is the fascinating dynamic between the self-expression of performers and what is often referred to as 'the demands of the material' attenuated – in favour of the performer in the former case and the performerless material in the latter. What is it that differentiates players from one another, what is it that makes listeners feel that some performers are more expressive than others, and what really is meant by the word 'expression' in the various circumstances in which music is played? Elvis Presley, Kathleen Ferrier, Billie Holiday, Paul Robeson, and Youssou N'Dour were or are musicians whose sound is immediately recognizable for large numbers of listeners, and who are highly distinctive as performers. In the case of singers (such as these five), this may be due in part to the specific timbre of their voices which is in turn a product of the size, shape, gender, nationality, and ethnicity of the individuals themselves. In other words, we *hear* the identity of these individuals as directly as we *see* it when shown photographs of them.

But the vocal identity of an individual is far more than just timbre: it is conveyed by the ways in which singers *use* their voices – how they pace their delivery, use vibrato and dynamics, slur or articulate words, and use purer or breathier tone – rather than what might be thought of as the 'raw sound'. This becomes more obvious when instrumental performers are considered, because the sound of the instrument itself is often not particularly distinctive. Miles Davis, Glenn Gould, and Jimi Hendrix used instruments that were more or less identical in their sound-making characteristics to those used by many other trumpeters, pianists, or electric guitarists, but what they *did* with that instrumental sound has made them highly recognizable.

The recognizable identity of a performer (their 'identifiability') is just one aspect of the broader question of what makes music expressive. The term *expression* is used to refer to both the characteristics of specific pieces (e.g. the Prelude in E minor by Chopin, Op. 28 no. 4, could be described as 'heartfelt and poignant') and the particular performance characteristics of specific individuals or groups. The first usage is often shorthand for claiming something about the emotional impact of certain music: arguing that Chopin's E minor Prelude is an expressive piece is more often than not a claim that people find it moving, irrespective of who plays it. When applied to a performer ('Jacqueline du Pré's playing is so expressive'), the implication is that whatever she plays will have an emotional impact. However, not every performance of the E minor Prelude is necessarily and inevitably 'expressive' (it could quite easily be played in mundane or even irritating ways) and Jacqueline du Pré is unlikely to have played equally expressively in every piece that she performed. Nevertheless some material arguably lends itself to expressive performance, and some individuals are perceived to be particularly drawn to expressive ways of playing. The question of whether certain kinds of musical materials are particularly expressive, and if so why, is something that we discuss in the next part of this book (see Chapter 6); here, we explore the nature of expression in performance.

3.1.1 **What is expression?**

Chiung-Hui is a music student who plays the clarinet. At her weekly lesson, she plays the first of Stravinsky's *Three Pieces* for solo clarinet to her teacher, who compliments her on having learned the notes and rhythms so quickly, but says that she now needs to 'play it with more expression'. Chiung-Hui has another go at it, bringing out more of the dynamic shaping and contrasts in her playing, and pulling around the tempo a bit more, particularly at the ends of phrases and in places where Stravinsky's slurring and breath marks indicate that she can take a bit of time. Her teacher says that it is fine, and much better, but to be careful neither to overdo the expression nor to slip into too predictable a pattern.

People learning an instrument in the classical tradition are often encouraged by their teachers to 'play with more expression' – but what does that actually mean, and how do players typically respond to such a request? They are most likely to play with larger numbers of more noticeable dynamic differences, greater and more frequent changes in articulation (the continuum between legato and staccato), more vibrato, and larger tempo fluctuations. Such responses provide a guide to what these players (and their teachers, assuming that the response satisfies them) think that expression means. Expression is the way in which a musician brings a piece to life, perhaps in a way that conveys his or her own personal interpretation of the music by manipulating certain aspects of the performance but which nonetheless leaves the piece recognizable and intact. This informal definition might seem reasonably uncontroversial, but it is important to recognize that it immediately aligns itself with a particular kind of musical tradition – one in which there are identifiable 'works'. Western art music is one such tradition (although not the only one, of course), and our discussion will start by confining itself to this specific context, before broadening out to consider the nature and function of expression in other musical traditions.

As Chiung-Hui's immediate response to her teacher shows, musicians seem to have a tacit understanding of what 'expression' means: the use of continuous variables of performance such as timing, dynamics, vibrato, timbre, articulation, or portamento to bring out the character of the piece. Changing patterns of dynamics or fluctuations in tempo, some of which may be indicated in the score, but only in very approximate terms, and some of which may have no explicit basis in the score itself, leaves Stravinsky's piece recognizably the same, while making more of it – increasing its vividness or interest. When Chiung-Hui does this, she conveys her own interpretation of an engagement with the music while leaving the identity of the piece untouched. But is Chiung-Hui really 'bringing out' something that, by implication, is somehow latent within the piece itself – or is she imposing something upon it? Where does this expressive transformation of the music come from, and what influences the specific way that it is realized?

Music psychologists have defined expression, typically, as transformations of, or deviations from fixed categories of musical events (fixed pitches, discrete rhythmic categories, distinct dynamic levels, and kinds of articulation).[1] As the overwhelming majority of research on expressive performance has focussed on Western art music, expression has often simply been defined as deviations from the explicit notation of the score. This definition has an intuitive appeal because it seems to draw a neat line between those attributes that the composer has explicitly indicated in the score, and those that the performer contributes – the identifiable aspects of a performance that are not explicitly marked in the score. But this apparently neat distinction raises questions that go right to the heart of what we mean by not only the term *expression* but also the idea of 'a piece of music'. For instance, how are we to distinguish between deliberate transformations and mistakes? If a clarinettist sustains a note beyond its notated length because she is momentarily unsure about the next note in the piece, how is this differentiated from a note that is prolonged for emotional impact or because it finishes a phrase? From the performer's perspective, the two circumstances are quite different, but from the listener's perspective they may seem difficult to tell apart – at least in principle. Thus minor accidents may be heard as expressive effects, and deliberately expressive gestures, particularly when executed awkwardly, may be heard as slips. And what about the different degrees of explicitness with which composers (and editors) notate their scores? If expression is defined in relation to the score, then a performer working from a score with very detailed expressive

---

[1] In a definition proposed in the 1930s, Carl Seashore (1938: 9) wrote that 'the artistic expression of feeling in music consists in esthetic deviation from the regular – from pure tone, true pitch, even dynamics, metronomic time, rigid rhythms, etc.' For further discussion of the definition of expression, see Alf Gabrielsson's (1999) encyclopaedic review chapter on music performance, and Clarke (2002).

markings might seem to have few expressive options whereas another performer working from a different edition of the same piece with fewer expressive markings, but producing exactly the same performance in acoustical terms, would be considered to be playing expressively! How are we to distinguish between general performance conventions and individual expressive characteristics? A convention of Baroque performance practice is to treat dotted rhythms in various ways (overdotting or underdotting, according to context) and to play pairs of quavers in a lilting long–short pattern, but it seems counter-intuitive to describe these widespread and predictable features as *expressive* features: they seem more like tacit conventions that it is assumed a competent score reader or performer will know.

These questions and apparent problems stem from too literal and score-based a definition of expression, and one way to overcome that difficulty, while retaining the idea of 'departure from a norm', is to understand the basic principle much more flexibly. Performers and listeners have more or less firm intuitions about compositional and performance conventions derived from exposure and experience, and their judgements of expressivity are based on a kind of play with these conventions or expectations. This idea, in one form or another, has been a feature of psychological theories of music for a long time: Leonard Meyer, for instance, argued that emotion and meaning in music arise from the setting up and thwarting of expectations derived largely from a tacit grasp of the norms or conventions of the particular musical style.[2] One of the apparent paradoxes of Meyer's theory is that listeners and performers continue to experience strong emotional responses to very familiar music, even though there should be little or nothing left to surprise them in the music – no expectations to be thwarted. One solution is to recognize the important distinction between the *literal* knowledge, or memory of what comes next in a piece or performance, and an underlying sense of what would *normally* have been expected within the conventions of the particular musical or performance style. The music psychologist Jamshed Bharucha has used

---

[2] The ideas were first developed by Meyer in two books (see Meyer, 1956, 1967).

the terms 'veridical' and 'schematic' expectancy, respectively, to pinpoint this distinction: veridical expectancies are based on a literal familiarity with the events (such as knowing that there is a pause on the fourth note of the first movement of Beethoven's Fifth Symphony); schematic expectancies are based on the general conventions of the style (for instance that at bar 11 of the same piece, after four bars of tonic harmony, the music is very likely to move to the dominant – as it does). The principle is closely related to the distinction between episodic (specific) and semantic (general) memory that was discussed in the last chapter. Episodic memories encode specific events that are often quite precisely located in time and place (e.g. what you had for breakfast the day before yesterday) whereas semantic memory provides a framework of generalizable knowledge that applies to an infinite number of individual situations (e.g. the linguistic or musical knowledge that allows you to make sense of a sentence, or a symphony, that you have never come across before).

Francisco is a pianist who has for many years been fascinated with Glenn Gould's recordings. He particularly loves Gould's second recording of J. S. Bach's *Goldberg Variations*, and specifically, the nuances of timing in his performance – every one of which he knows intimately from repeated listening to that much-loved recording. In the mid 1980s, Francisco knew little of 'historically informed' performance practice, but vividly remembers the first time he heard a Haydn sonata played on an 18th century fortepiano – and how strange and stimulating that whole approach to keyboard expression and sound then seemed. He now feels much less excited by that type of playing, and listening to the recordings from that period, he finds it hard to imagine what it was that seemed so interesting and expressive.

In relation to performance expression, the principle of schematic expectancy explains how a recorded performance, such as Gould's recording of the *Goldberg Variations* can continue to sound expressive even after hundreds of hearings, because it still does not conform to the norms of what might be called 'standard' performance. Even a perfect episodic memory of the performance still fails to resolve the ways in which the timing and articulation of the performance differ from the schematic norms embodied within semantic memory. By contrast, the first time that Francisco encountered the sound and style of historically informed performance, he had neither episodic nor semantic knowledge to prepare him for the unexpected patterns of timing, dynamics, and timbre that he heard. With repeated exposure to that style of playing, the norms and conventions of the approach have become firmly established in Francisco's semantic memory, and what at first seemed striking now seems to him predictable and even routine.

3.1.2 Characteristics of expression

If variations of timing, dynamics, and articulation (and other parameters of performance) can become predictable to listeners and performers, then they must conform to some kind of systematic patterning, and a great deal of music performance research has tried to discover what those patterns are like, and what kind of psychological process could account for them. Since the very first empirical studies of performance, it has been obvious that expressive performances show an impressive degree of consistency, both within the piece being played (for example when the same, or similar passages are repeated) and when it is played by the same performer on different occasions, perhaps many years apart. It is implausible on psychological and musical grounds to imagine that performers memorize and then simply reproduce a complicated pattern of expressive features for every piece that they play: the memory load would be astronomical for even quite a simple piece, and the idea does not explain where the patterns come from in the first place. The more obvious solution is that these patterns are closely related to the structure of the musical material, and that they are generated from that structure at the time of performance, just as the patterns of stress, timing, and pitch inflection in speech are generated 'online' as part of the speaker's overall communicative aim. Rather like Tim's largely improvized performance discussed in the previous chapter, there isn't really a memory component at all in this aspect of a performance unless a performer deliberately wants to play a piece in exactly the same way that he or she did on some previous occasion. The consistency (and flexibility) of expression is understood instead as a consequence of a stable (or flexible) view of what and where the important events in the music are. If that remains constant, then the expressive profile remains constant too; if the conception changes, then so does the expression.

A large body of research has therefore investigated the features of musical structure that are primarily responsible for influencing or even driving performance expression, and the ways in which tempo fluctuation, dynamic changes, vibrato, articulation, and so on are shaped.[3] The typical behaviours of a Western classical music performer are summarized in the following:

> ### Common features of expression in the performance of Western classical music
>
> - Slow up towards phrase endings, accelerate towards the middle of phrases.
> - Get quieter towards phrase endings, louder towards the middle.
> - Emphasize significant or unexpected events (e.g. at harmonic changes) by playing them louder (or suddenly softer), or longer, or with different articulation, or different timbre, or more (or less!) vibrato, or by delaying them slightly.
> - In multipart music, bring out the most salient line by playing it louder, or desynchronizing it slightly in relation to other lines, or by using a different timbre for it.
> - Emphasize rhythmic distinctions by playing long notes longer and short notes shorter.
> - Emphasize metrical structure by making recurrent dynamic and/or timing distinctions between different beats.

---

[3] Some examples of this approach are Todd (1985), Clarke (1988), and Sundberg (1988). Discussion of some of the problems of a structure-based view can be found in Clarke (2002).

Phrase structure is the most widely reported structural characteristic associated with performance expression, which seems intuitively plausible for two reasons: it is what performers tend to refer to when they talk about the 'shaping' of a performance; and as a structural entity, the phrase brings together many components of musical structure (such as rhythm, harmony, motivic structure, textural change) and channels their influence into expressive shaping. In very general terms, expressive features are used to articulate phrase boundaries and the shape or direction of phrases – so that performers typically slow up and get quieter towards phrase endings, and get faster and louder towards the middle of phases – and do so in a manner that reflects the structural importance of the phrase: the effects tend to be more pronounced at more structurally significant points in the music. Performers may also use changes of articulation (along the continuum between smooth *legato* playing and spiky or *staccato* playing), or the amount of vibrato they use, in a similar way.

What psychological principles lie behind this shaping of timing, dynamics, articulation, and other features relative to the structure of the music? Is it just a particular historical convention to slow up towards a phrase boundary, or does it serve some specific psychological purpose? Does the specific shape of the expressive change matter, or does it just act like a kind of musical highlighter pen, marking out the structure, but in an arbitrary 'colour' (so to speak) against the 'black and white' of the basic material? Some of the research in this area has indicated the close relationship between musical expression and physical movement.[4] For example when performers slow up towards the end of a piece, section, or phrase it has been claimed that they use a pattern of deceleration that mirrors that of runners coming to a stop at the end of a race, or the swinging of a pendulum as it reaches its point of maximum displacement. When 'artificial' (e.g. computer-generated)

---

[4] For ideas about the relationship between music and movement see Shove & Repp (1995); Clarke & Davidson (1998); Todd (1999); Johnson & Larson (2003); and Gjerdingen (1999). The psychologist Johan Sundberg has argued that the *ritardando* in music is related to the timing pattern of footsteps when a runner slows down and stops: see Sundberg & Verillo (1980); and Kronman & Sundberg (1987).

performances use these particular timing curves, they tend to sound more convincing than when they use some arbitrary acceleration or deceleration function. This underlines the physical and instrumental character of performance and expression. Playing music is an intensely physical activity, and it is inevitable that the physicality both of the performers' bodies and of the instruments that they play will be manifest in the sound patterns that are produced. The micropauses between phrases are tied up with the physical control of musical production (for example pausing to take a breath, or change bow, or change hand position on the keyboard), as well as with matters of interpretation and communication, and all music-making involves a fascinating and complex interplay between the constraints and opportunities offered by musical instruments in relation to the human body, and the aesthetic and communicative aims of the players. Playing music expressively is not just a matter of abstract musical reasoning translated into sound.

There are also strong similarities between the expressive features of musical performance and the expressive properties of everyday speech, and it seems certain that some of the same psychological principles underlie both. As an example, imagine speaking the sentence 'Francisco loves Gould's *Goldberg* recording' five times, putting the main emphasis on each of the words in turn, and consider how each version changes what is conveyed by the sentence. With the emphasis on 'Francisco', for example, the implication is that he does but that others do not, and with the emphasis on 'recording', the implication might be that although he loves the recording, he once heard Gould play live and did not think much of it. These prosodic features of speech (as they are called) serve to highlight certain meanings at the expense of others, break up the flow of information so as to give listeners a chance to understand and take stock of what they have heard, can convey a variety of rhetorical attitudes (e.g. irony, conviction, concern), and make continuities or disjunctions between different sections of the whole utterance. Despite significant differences between language and music, very similar functions using broadly the same means are found in music.

Musical performances are not just auditory phenomena, and in an age when we have become used to hearing music from sound recordings, it can be easy to forget how important the visual aspects of performance are, whether the performance is live, or on TV or DVD. Perception involves a complex interaction between different sensory modalities (hearing, sight, touch, smell, taste), and the information conveyed by one sensory channel is often closely intertwined with that conveyed by another. The apparent confidence or anxiety, expressiveness or coldness, projection or introversion, and assertiveness or accommodation of a musician's playing comes across in how they look (their posture, movement, facial expressions and even style of dress) as well as how they sound. Some of this use of the body may be closely linked to the simple ergonomics of playing an instrument (it is hard not to move around quite energetically if you play drums in a rock band), but a lot of it seems to be much more related to either an unconscious expression of a player's response to the music or a deliberate attempt to communicate a particular expressive attitude. The variably strutting or sensuous actions of the front men or women in pop bands (think of Mick Jagger, Madonna, or Jarvis Cocker) are a mixture of the unconscious consequences of their intentions to put across a song in a particular way, and a much more deliberately choreographed component that has been explicitly worked out and rehearsed. Performers in other traditions may be less extravagant in their stage demeanour, but their appearance and body movements are no less expressively important. Using video recordings of performers, and in some cases deliberately manipulating the relationship between the sound track and the visual track, Jane Davidson has shown how influential these body movements can be in performance, and how they involve both rather general components, such as the more or less continuous swaying of an instrumentalist, and more discrete local gestures that seem to convey the function or significance of particular events in the music.[5] Here, again, there seems to be a commonality with language: many of the kinds of gestures found in musical performance are also found in the non-verbal components of speech, suggesting that they may have deep-rooted origins in pervasive

---

[5] For accounts of different aspects of this work, see Davidson (2001, 2002) and Davidson and Correia (2002).

cultural conventions and/or in the biology of the body, and in particular, the ways in which the body makes emotional states visible and audible.

3.1.3 Emotion and expression

> Alice is the singer in a Velvet Underground tribute band. The band are rehearsing the set for a gig the following night, and are not happy with how it is going. One of the other band members suggests that the whole effect is not nearly 'remote and moody' enough and that the sound has to be much bleaker and more alienated. They try again, and Alice sings with a thinner and more menacing sound. The result is much more along the right lines – and they all agree that the music now sounds appropriately 'scary'.

It would be easy to get the impression from the previous sections that expression in performance is largely concerned with communicating 'the music'. But a conversation with a performer in almost any musical tradition would reveal how central emotional engagement is to what they do. When Alice changes the expressive aspects of her vocal delivery, she is not thinking about phrase structures and harmonic functions but about how to create or convey a particular emotional character. The emotions that are communicated might be different from those that she is feeling at the time, a distinction (between emotions conveyed and emotions felt) that is discussed in Chapter 6.

The factors involved in emotional expression and communication have been studied by asking musicians to play or sing relatively neutral musical material so as to convey one of a small number of specific emotions. For instance, a guitar player might be asked to play 'When The Saints' in a manner that conveys fear, her performance being analysed acoustically to see what makes a performance sound 'fearful' and also recorded and played to a separate group of listeners to assess how successful her performance is in conveying the emotion. This research shows that with simple materials and a small number of basic emotions (happy, sad, angry, fearful), predictable acoustical changes can be seen in the performances, and listeners are very successful in identifying the intended emotion. A performance that is intended to convey fear, for example, tends to be played at a low dynamic, with staccato articulation, and an irregular rhythm. Once again, there are clear connections here with both speech and the use of the body more generally: the speech patterns of a fearful speaker are likely to show characteristics that are more or less identical to those described here, just as the movements of a person fearfully approaching another person or object are also likely to be restrained ($\approx$ low dynamic), hesitant ($\approx$ irregular rhythm), and lacking in fluency ($\approx$ staccato).

This account, however, runs the risk of treating expression in a naively 'naturalistic' and essentialized manner. Recordings from different times and places demonstrate that expressive performance cannot be divorced from its cultural and historical context. Historical recordings of classical music are particularly interesting, because although the musical materials are constant, the performance styles can be radically different. There is also a danger of regarding structure, emotion, bodily movement and instrumental design as though they are separate factors, each of which influences performance, but which operate independently of one another. In fact, the opposite is the case: musical structure, performance conventions, the emotional 'narrative' that a performer discovers or invents, the possibilities and limitations of the instrument, and the performer's own physical engagement with it are all tightly bound together in a complex web of interactions, as the psychologist Patrik Juslin has tried to indicate in a model of expressive performance.[6] Musicians also, of course, inhabit a world that is saturated with the sounds of other players, under different expectations of conformism or innovation depending on the cultural context within which they operate, and thus with a whole range of pressures to adopt, or resist adopting, what they hear around them. In some traditional musical cultures (for example, Vedic chant, from the Indian subcontinent), it is not just acceptable but even a *requirement* to perpetuate and preserve the detailed conventions of performance, whereas in others (such as the

---

6 See Juslin et al. (2001–2002), and Juslin (2003).

concert music of the West), the equal and opposite pressure is constantly to assert one's distinctive musical identity through innovative performance.

The social context, and social nature of expression are even more apparent, at a micro level, when group performance is considered. Despite its prominence in the research literature, solo performance is arguably the exception rather than the rule, and the interactions that can be observed in group performance provide a fascinating opportunity to study the ways in which expressive choices are formulated, negotiated, and agreed upon. The solitary processes by which solo performers arrive at interpretative decisions are difficult to study, unless the performers happen to be particularly articulate and skilled at introspecting. The interactions between members of string quartets, jazz ensembles, or samba bands, however, make such processes somewhat more explicit. Although the cognitive mechanisms that are responsible for the coordination between the two hands of a pianist have to be inferred from the timing characteristics or errors of a performance, the problems of coordination among the members of an ensemble, and their proposed solutions, can be observed much more directly through the difficulties that they identify ('you're always late coming in after my solo') and the strategies that they adopt ('listen out for my high note and get ready to come in right after that' vs. 'watch out and I'll give you a nod'). In short, when groups of musicians are rehearsing, there is likely to be rather more talk than when soloists practise (unless they have been asked to provide verbal commentaries for the purposes of research), and there may well also be more physical interaction to observe and analyse.

Summary

What do performers do, and what can a broadly psychological perspective reveal about their performances? Playing music at a high level represents a remarkable human achievement in terms of the combination of skills that it requires – physical, cognitive, interpretative, social, and emotional. In the reality of playing music, these separable components are all thoroughly intertwined, but as this chapter and the last have demonstrated, it is interesting and revealing to try to tease apart their different contributions. On the one hand, there are those skills that are required to live up to the demands of playing music: the ability to produce with precision and independence the movements that most instruments require; the capacity to read, remember, or create the material to be performed; the control of time and coordination with others that music typically involves; and the capacity to cope with, and enjoy, the adrenaline of public performance. On the other hand, there are the skills that players deploy to stamp their personalities on performance, and to bring the music that they play to life: their expressive responses to the musical material; what might be called their performance 'rhetoric' – conveyed in facial expressions and movement, as well as sound; and their ability to detect and react appropriately to the intentions of their co-performers, and to engage an audience. Building on existing theories of motor control, timing, memory, perception, the focus of attention, the nature of expression, and the relationship between vision and audition, psychological research has shed light on a human activity that carries considerable cultural value in many human societies; conversely, musical performance offers a fascinating domain in which to develop psychological explanations of the complex relationship between individual expertise and social interaction.

Chapter 4

Improvising and composing

We can think of 'making music' as lying on a continuum from the completely rigid reproduction of a fixed model to totally spontaneous creation out of thin air. Neither end of this continuum can really be reached: even with so-called fixed-medium electronic music (music made on a computer, stored in digital memory or on a disk, and then played over a sound system), there are still one or two 'degrees of freedom', even if the only choices the diffuser has to make are when to start the sequence of events and at what amplitude to diffuse them.[1] Equally, spontaneous creation is a fiction: a free improviser always starts from some state of consciousness in which there is *some* residual influence of previous events, or starting point, and must perform within a set of technical and aesthetic constraints and possibilities that have become part of his or her history. As we have already observed, the Western art music tradition, and some other notated or rigidly ceremonial traditions, make a firm distinction between playing and creating, but in the great majority of the world's musical activities, there is a much more fluid relationship between the two. Improvisation involves both, to greater or lesser extent, and having spent much of the last two chapters considering playing, we now turn to improvising and its close cousin, composing.

4.1 Improvising

Rachel (1st violin), Yoshitaka (2nd violin), Pedro (viola), and Anna (cello) are performing Beethoven's String Quartet in A minor, Op. 132, in a public concert. It's been in their repertoire for nearly eight years and they've performed it six times in the last four months,

---

[1] In practice, fixed-medium music of this kind often features continuous manipulation of various aspects of the sound, such as spatialization and balance, during live diffusion.

but Pedro is surprised to hear Anna use distinctly more vibrato and a richer sound than usual in her first entry. Reacting quickly, he plays his two answering notes with more and less vibrato in turn, and Yoshitaka and Rachel, coming in successively on the next two notes, take up and intensify this drier and more restrained quality. At the beginning of Bar 5 where all four instruments play together for the first time, with the tacit understanding of an established ensemble, they achieve a kind of washed-out and remote sound quality that seems (to them) exactly right for this performance – an expressive contrast to the more robust start, but something that the quartet has never tried to do before …

At about the same time, the jazz pianist Nikki Iles and her trio are starting their first set of the night with a rather spiky rendering of Bill Evans' 'Blue in Green'. The drummer, Anthony Michelli, responds to Nikki's upward-jumping, fragmented line with some restrained snare and ride cymbal, waiting his turn to break out with more demonstrative playing once she in turn has pulled back a little on her solo.

Improvisation in music might be loosely defined as the art of 'making it up as you go along' – but is there really a difference between the two performance situations imagined above? The pitches, rhythms, and general dynamic markings of the string quartet performance may be laid down in the parts from which the four performers play, but almost everything to do with pacing, detailed dynamic shaping, timbre, vibrato, and the precise synchronization of each instrument as it enters the texture is 'made up' by the players in the course of the performance. By comparison, the pattern of notes and rhythms in Nikki Iles' solo may not be laid down in advance, but having played this Bill Evans tune 200 times or more in her career, she draws on a common stock of phrases, licks, and general patterns of melodic construction in each performance. These two kinds of music-making have more in common than might at first be thought.

Within a broadly Western conception, although not only in this context, improvisation occupies an intermediate position between performance and composition and, as the improviser Derek Bailey has put it, 'enjoys the curious distinction of being the most widely practised of all musical activities and the least acknowledged and understood. Defined in any one of a series of catchphrases ranging from 'making it up as he goes along' to 'instant composition', improvisation is generally viewed as a musical conjuring trick, a doubtful expedient, or even a vulgar habit.'[2] Using the language of computer science, improvisation has often been characterized as 'online' creation, and composition as its 'offline' counterpart, but the metaphor arguably conceals as much as it reveals. It is true that improvisation involves a significant degree of moment-by-moment creativity of the most obvious kind: Nikki Iles sets out on her solo with perhaps little more than a harmonic framework in mind together with some fragments of the tune of 'Blue in Green'. In the course of her solo, she produces hundreds – perhaps thousands – of musical events that seem to come from nowhere, and an obvious focus for psychological research on improvisation has been to ask where those events come from. Again, the parallel with language seems obvious: if you want to tell someone how great it was to walk to the top of Arthur's Seat in Edinburgh late one summer evening, or how frustrating it was to miss the bus on the way home, you will find the words to describe those events and emotions there and then, rather than reciting a rehearsed speech. That is what everyday 'improvised' discourse is like. But not every utterance will be novel: you will almost certainly find yourself using the common turns of phrase and ways of organizing such a description that are not set down anywhere but are nevertheless shared by your linguistic or cultural community, and if

---

2 This comes from the Introduction (p. ix) of Derek Bailey's (1992) fascinating book on improvisation. After a long period in which improvisation was largely ignored in academic or analytical writing, there has been increasing interest in trying to make sense of it from both psychological and ethnomusicological perspectives. See, for instance, Pressing (1988), Berliner (1994), Monson (1996), Sawyer (1997), and Nettl and Russell (1998).

you find yourself using just a few too many stock phrases you may begin to feel that your account sounds a little clichéd.

In many ways, musical improvisation shares a great deal with this kind of everyday linguistic experience, and because there is a very long tradition in linguistics of explaining the structured creativity of everyday speaking and writing in terms of the framework of grammar, it seems reasonable to see if the same kind of approach might help to understand improvisation in music. When the musical style is relatively constrained (such as playing a 12-bar blues), this approach seems to have quite a bit to offer: just as grammar provides the structure into which an infinite variety of different utterances can fit, so too an infinite variety of specific improvisations, with different rhythms, melodies, harmonies, and all the expressive attributes described in Chapter 3 can be generated within the 12-bar framework. The 'grammar' account can help to explain in a purely structural sense how it is that an improviser keeps track of where he or she is, and how a listener makes sense of what is going on, but seems much less helpful in understanding where the specific events come from.

As in the discussion of expression in Chapter 3, the question of what underlies improvisation becomes less puzzling when two important factors are taken into account: the relationship between the body and the instrument, and the social context of music. If improvisation is regarded as abstract decision making, the listener may well ask where all those notes come from, and in particular, how they all get there so quickly. Improvising musicians play just as fast as their score-reading counterparts, so however they do it, they must be making or finding the material with incredible speed. One explanation relates to the physicality of instrumental performance: instruments have a kind of 'grain' to them – lines of least resistance, as it were, whereby the physical design of the instrument, understood in relation to the properties of the human body, makes certain patterns of events so easy to accomplish that they almost 'fall out' of the body–instrument interaction, while others are much more unlikely. Analyses of even some of the most original improvisers, such as the saxophonist Charlie Parker, have shown that important attributes of their improvisations can be explained by considering the layout of the instrument (in the case of Charlie Parker, the saxophone keys) in relation to the body (Parker's hands). This clearly is not the whole story, otherwise piano improvisations would always sound like five-finger exercises, but it certainly challenges the idea that improvising is a kind of problem-solving. Jazz musicians have talked about how their 'fingers seem to do the thinking',[3] an experience that seems to stem from a combination of the performer's repertoire of highly over-learned riffs and licks (many jazz musicians spend a great deal of time practising characteristic melodic patterns and motivic units that are good ways of getting from A to B), a knowledge of the circumstances in which they are appropriate, and simple ergonomics.

It is also vital to remember that jazz, like most other improvising traditions, is a social phenomenon, and that its basic material is distributed within the collective consciousness or 'cultural memory' of a community, rather than being either the property or the product of an individual. If jazz improvisation consisted only of stringing together riffs and licks, it would be like the 'improvisation' of a second-rate stand-up comedian who tells the same jokes every night in a different, but still essentially arbitrary order – and it may be that the formulaic playing of bored or disenchanted improvisers does indeed resemble this. Good improvisers, however, produce much more interesting performances. Jazz, in particular, is an idiom in which players, living and dead, are much more important than 'pieces', and one consequence of this (at least in some kinds of jazz) is that players pay homage to those who have influenced them by adopting elements of their style. Their playing thus avoids becoming formulaic because typically a player will drop in one of these references in a place and manner that makes the sideways reference clear: Nikki Iles might drop a little scrap of a Thelonius Monk tune into the middle of her playing both to 'pay her respects' and at the same time to turn the improvising in a particular direction. A skilled and

---

[3] Berliner's (1994) seminal book on jazz provides examples of these and many other insights derived from copious interviews and conversations with professional jazz musicians.

fluent improvisation therefore takes place in a context – one might almost say a landscape – in which many factors converge, and through which the improviser steers a course: the harmonic outline, physicality of the instrument and body, references to the 'player legacy', and the influence throughout the performance of the other players in the band.

The kind of improvising described so far is that of the skilled and deliberate improviser, working within a structured context. But there are many other kinds of improvisation that should not be overlooked, including so-called free improvisation, and the informal, private, and pervasive semi-improvisation that goes on when people hum to themselves at the bus stop or sing as they cycle to work. Free improvisation (which is actually something of a misnomer) highlights a social component in music making that is nearly always there, but which is perhaps easier to overlook in less 'free' forms of music making. When an obvious style framework regulates improvisation, the interpersonal dynamics of an ensemble tend to be either more systematically regulated, or paradoxically partially concealed, by the formal structure through which they are negotiated. For example the characteristic pattern of bebop (head tune, followed by a succession of solo improvisations, concluding with the head tune played again) controls both the overall musical pattern and certain crucial roles that the players in the ensemble act out in relation to one another. But take away those formal structures and the resulting music seems suddenly to expose, and depend on, those interpersonal interactions much more obviously. If precomposed music seems to determine certain kinds of social relationships (a symphonic work for orchestra, and a violin sonata seem to imply, and perhaps require, very different kinds of interpersonal interactions), then free improvisation could be seen as its counterpart: a set of interpersonal relationships (a certain group of people who have come together in a particular playing environment) that has a particular kind of music as its outcome.[4]

---

[4] For further discussion of this and related ideas about improvisation, see Monson (1996), Cook (2004), and Clarke (2005a).

It is a sunny day, and Sam is waiting on her own at a bus stop. A man comes out of the adjacent bank and stands a little awkwardly, also waiting for the bus, humming something that sounds to Sam like a modified fragment of Gershwin's 'Summertime' – as if to let Sam know that he is there (he is standing behind her and she has not turned around, so she might not have noticed that she is no longer alone), and to fill the awkward silence of two strangers waiting together.

Where has this humming man's music come from, who has 'made' it, and should we consider it to be composed and performed, or improvised? Situations such as the one described above are familiar and widespread, but again raise questions as to where the boundaries fall between the various kinds of 'making' music presented in this and the previous chapters. We could identify the composer of this music as Gershwin and the performer as the humming man, but these definitions do not capture what is really going on. It is far more likely that the humming man does not know that 'Summertime' is by Gershwin, and that he is just humming the tune that has popped into his mind perhaps triggered by the sunny day and an unconscious association with the half-thought word 'summer'. The source of the music, then, is a more or less partial episodic memory (i.e. a specific pitch-time profile), which is elaborated and extended in the course of the humming by means of this man's semantic memory, the limits of his humming expertise (the tune spans an octave in its first ten notes, so if he happened to start a bit low, he might spontaneously change the melody so as to stay within the range of comfortable hummability), and adjustments to, or rationalizations of, any accidental mishummings as he goes along. This is definitely improvisation, in the same way that most everyday conversations are, but with the purpose not of producing a musical performance but rather of achieving a different and more practical social function.

If the humming man represents the most informal, and perhaps least deliberate, manifestation of 'making music', then improvisational showpieces – exemplified by J. S. Bach demonstrating his improvising prowess to Frederick the Great, using a theme given to him by the king – are the most formal and rarefied, and are the most closely allied to composition. Bach was reputedly dissatisfied with his improvised fugue and almost immediately set about trying to do justice to the original challenge – to improvise a fugue based on the given theme – through composition rather than improvisation, which became what is now known as the *Musical Offering*. What Bach apparently felt that he was not able to achieve in the 'online' context of improvisation, he certainly accomplished in its 'offline' counterpart.[5]

4.2 Composing

The study of composition affords an insight into a particular kind of cultural creation that has fascinated people for centuries, and has generated all manner of extraordinary stories and cultural myths, and a window on to human creativity more generally. Such insight, of course, is not easy to obtain. According to the stereotype of the Western classical composer, the tortured genius struggles with his (nearly always 'his' in the stereotype) muse and then, almost miraculously, pours forth the inspired result. How can anyone possibly investigate the cognitive processes underlying this achievement? The stereotype is of course just that – created and bolstered by countless discourses around Western art music, which have sought to elevate composition to the status of a mystical and quasi-religious phenomenon – and for some time now, it has been recognized that even those composers who seem to conform to it (Mozart, for instance) actually left rather more in the way of traces of their creative activity than the myths might suggest.

Those traces are the obvious place to start investigating the creative process, and where composers (Beethoven and Stravinsky among them) left extensive sketches much can be gleaned about the changes they made as they worked; the aesthetic or other motivations that drove those changes can also be inferred from their sketches and other written evidence. Living composers, of course, can be studied more

---

[5] A fictional account of what the improvising encounter, and subsequent spur to composition, might have been like is provided in James Gaines' (2005) book *Evening in the Palace of Reason. Bach Meets Frederick the Great in the Age of Enlightenment.*

directly: John Sloboda is unusual in that he is a psychologist who also has experience as a composer, and in his 1985 book *The Musical Mind*, he provides a rare example of sustained writing on the psychological processes underlying composition.[6] His discussion includes an introspective account that fills in a gap that is necessarily a characteristic of the traditional 'sketch study' approach – namely, the thought processes that lie behind, or run in parallel with, the manifest features that are left on the paper. The work in question was a choral piece and as he composed a passage of about 30 bars in length, he tried to tease out his own mental processes in what is known as a 'talk-aloud verbal protocol'. Reflecting both the dominant cognitive approach of that time and perhaps Sloboda's own intellectual predispositions, the account concentrates largely on the problem-solving aspect of this complex process – something that is undoubtedly an important part of composition but arguably *only* a part. Other aspects might have included his awareness of the influence of other composers' pieces or styles, his knowledge of the capacities of the performers for whom the work was either intended or ideally imagined, the space in which it would be heard and occasion on which it would be performed, the function it would fulfil, pressures of kudos and reputation, and so on.

Introspection is a rich but problematic source of information. Indeed, a significant factor in the development of modern experimental psychology was the recognition that introspection could not form the primary basis for a scientific psychology: it has no access (by definition) to the unconscious processes that play a crucial role in human behaviour and mental life; it is subject to the conscious or unconscious 'rationalizations' and distortions of the introspectors themselves – at best biasing its insights, at worst rendering them fatally suspect; and the process of

---

6 See Chapter 4 of Sloboda (1985), and also Chapter 7 of Lehmann et al. (2007). An ambitious collaboration between the American composer Roger Reynolds and the psychologist Stephen McAdams and colleagues is reported in a special issue of *Music Perception* (vol. 22, no.2, 2004), and in Reynolds's (2002) own writings about the nature and process of composition. Other writing on composition from a broadly psychological perspective includes a provocative article by the composer and theorist Fred Lerdahl (1988) that discusses the psychological 'reality' of different compositional systems, and a paper by composer Fabrice Fitch and cellist Neil Heyde (2007) that discusses their collaboration on a new composition.

introspection itself can dramatically interfere with the very process on which it is supposed to shed light (imagine trying to introspect on how you avoid having an accident on the motorway while actually trying to avoid having an accident on the motorway...). The results of introspective methods for studying creative processes are thus likely to be unreliable, so in recent years attempts have been made to study composition in real time by less intrusive and subjective means, making the most of changes in technology. The increasing use of desktop computers for composition, using either notation software or digital sound-editing software, opens up the possibility of keeping non-intrusive and continuous records of what composers do as they work. These are the modern equivalent of sketches, but they have the added virtue of revealing all the 'actions' of a composer – the amount of time spent on generating and changing material, the frequency with which material is 'tested by ear' or deleted, equivalent to rubbing out or throwing away whole pages – that conventional sketch studies tend to be unable to recover.[7] While the study of such records appears to be an improvement on the study of sketches, it remains an open question whether the data available for analysis in this explicit record of activity are any more than 'symptoms' of the far richer and more complex thought processes of the composer, that lie below the surface.

> Alex and Hussein are at a COMA (Contemporary Music Making for Amateurs) summer school, and are involved in a group-composition and improvisation session with 12 other musicians. They are working on an ensemble piece that will be played at the end of the week-long course. The brief they have been given by the course tutors is pretty open, but Hussein has an idea that he would like the piece to be about 10 minutes long and fairly spacious in terms of texture. The 14 musicians have had a go at improvising along those lines, but Alex

---

[7] David Collins (2005) gives an account of just such a study, which combines computer-based records with audio recordings and verbal protocol analysis. The paper also includes a concise discussion of, and extensive references to, the larger literature of research into composition and creative thinking.

is unhappy about the result: it reminds her too much of the kind of directionless 'texture' pieces with which she has never had much sympathy. She wants to try to achieve something much terser and less 'easy listening' – particularly because a composer friend of hers will be in the audience at the final concert. She proposes to the group that they devise a few pitch cells, or motivic fragments, that can be the basis of the piece and will stop them just riding around on their own musical hobby horses.

The 'private' character of individual composition presents particular kinds of difficulties, but a different perspective on composition – as with performance – is made possible by looking at what happens in the interactions between the members of groups who compose together. Pop musicians have been studied in this way, as described by Lucy Green in *How Popular Musicians Learn*,[8] as have children composing in groups, both in the context of formal music education and more informal situations. While the internal dialogue and decision-making that take place in a solitary composer's mind may be rather different from those that take place in groups, the advantage of studying group composition, from the researcher's point of view, is that processes likely to be hidden or implicit when studied in an individual composer become explicit when studied in a group of individuals who have to verbalise their aims, motivations, preferences, and working methods to one another.

Finally, it is worth recognizing that composition is the most obvious manifestation of creativity in music, and as such has been the object of more general psychological theories of creativity. Creativity has been studied from many different perspectives using computational, psychometric, cognitive, psychodynamic, social-psychological, and systems-theory approaches.[9] Once again, the emphasis in this literature

---

[8] Lucy Green's (2001) book *How Popular Musicians Learn: A Way Ahead for Music Education* provides detailed accounts of the ways in which a number of pop musicians acquired their skills, knowledge, and musical creativity in the informal contexts that tend to characterize the culture of popular music.

[9] For a wide-ranging treatment of this topic, see the collection of chapters in Robert Sternberg's (1999) edited book entitled the *Handbook of Creativity*.

is overwhelmingly on individual creativity, and as a result, it tends to be concerned more with the products of creativity, because they are observable, than with the processes that go into it, which are less so. This in turn is a function of the prevailing Romantic view of creativity - of aesthetic objects that emerge mysteriously from the inspired intuition of a gifted individual. An alternative view of creativity is to see it as an interactive process, the consequence of social circumstances and the material scaffolding of culture, without altogether discarding the recognition that for a variety of reasons some individuals are predisposed and/or enabled to exploit those circumstances more effectively than others.

To conclude, we still have a lot to learn about how people make music when improvising and composing. Improvisation is perhaps easier to investigate than the very private process of composition, as we have seen, and for this reason research on improvisation has sometimes substituted for research on composition. Improvisation itself, however, is a complex and multifaceted process. Ergonomic as well as cognitive factors explain how improvisers generate and produce musical material on their instruments, while social and aesthetic factors shape an improviser's style. At a more mundane level, most of us are improvisers as we hum, sing, or play our way through life – if we aren't now, we certainly were as infants – and there is thus, potentially, a rich body of data all around us for future analysis. The study of the cognitive and social processes underlying composition also has considerable unrealised potential. It may have been hampered in the past by researchers' preoccupations with the composition of Western art music – fascinating though this is – and it may be that a more tractable and equally interesting enterprise would be to look at those kinds of collaborative or semi-improvised composition by pop bands and songwriters that are more obviously observable.

Summary

Almost everyone makes music in one way or another at some point in their life, and many people invest huge amounts of time and energy in doing so over the whole of their lifespan. A wide range of psychological questions are raised by these music-making activities, from the motivations to start doing so, to the nature of the specific skills that may be required. Psychological research has made significant progress towards understanding at least some of these phenomena, and there is now a rich and substantial literature on musical performance, for example. Psychologists have tended to consider the mind as an individual attribute rather than the product of relationships between individuals, and between individuals and their environments, both natural and cultural. As a consequence, making music has been seen in terms of *individual* motivations, skills, interpretation, expressive power, communication, and creativity. But every kind of making involves social and material factors, and often, these are just as, if not more important. The saxophonist Charlie Parker, for example, widely recognized as one of the great innovators in jazz, did not dream up music in the abstract. He played a particular instrument with certain very salient physical characteristics, in a social and historical context that surrounded him with other musicians, managers, promoters, recordings, expectations and ideologies, financial pressures, and much more besides – all of which played their part, whether enabling or disabling, in the music that he made. It is impossible to take all of this into account all of the time, but after a period in which the focus of psychologists has been relatively narrow, orientated for the most part towards the cognitive processes believed to underlie the skills of Western classical musicians, there is increasing recognition by researchers of the advantages of looking also at a wider range of music-making, in the richly messy and varied contexts of its everyday reality.

Part 2

Using music

Music's 'uses' are apparent everywhere – whether as a source of fun or spiritual fulfilment, as a means to provide aural privacy in a crowd or conversely a bond between people, as a means of attracting the right kinds of customers or repelling vandals, the list is seemingly endless. The idea that music is socially instrumental is controversial for many people. From their perspective, 'using' music for its perceived 'effects' upon people is to do music and society a disservice, because music's value lies in its apparent 'functionlessness'. For this reason, 'using' music, as we employ the term here, encompasses not only the deliberate deployment of music to serve specific ends (for example, playing a CD to stay alert on a long car journey) but also instances which seem to lack an explicitly instrumental use (such as attending a concert). This section explores different ways of using music, and their biological, psychological, and social consequences. Chapter 5 examines the approach to listening that is most often applied to art music – namely, that music has an intrinsically musical use, which is sometimes characterized as 'structural listening' or 'art for art's sake'. Chapters 6 and 7 then go on to explore situations in which music is deliberately deployed for specific ends, focusing on individual (Chapter 6) and group processes (Chapter 7) – although in practice, as will become clear, the individual and social are inextricably intertwined.

Chapter 5

Hearing and listening

5.1 Hearing music and listening to music as using music

What does it mean to 'use music for its own sake'? One answer is the kind of activity that is often taken as the paradigm of listening to music: the concentrated listening that takes place at live musical events in concert halls or opera houses, or at home with recorded music heard over loudspeakers or headphones, in which the sonic properties of music seem to be the primary focus of attention. This mode of listening has been facilitated by the development of recording and playback technologies that allow music to be experienced away from its place and time of performance. On some occasions it might be appropriate and desirable to hear music with focused attention, as in the examples above, but at others sustained attentive listening might be counterproductive (as in the case of a person in a lively bar who attends solely to the music and ignores their friends) or unrewarding (as in the case of attentive listening to telephone ring tones). This distinction between 'active' or 'focused' listening and 'passive' or 'background' hearing is a theoretical simplification, and auditory experience often shifts between varieties of listening that may not always fit neatly into either of them. The distinction is also captured in the different, and sometimes problematically polarizing, connotations of the two words – 'hearing' and 'listening' – in general English language usage. However, conceptualizing listening in terms of these two modes provides a framework for thinking about the different things that people might hear in music, and what that might do for them. So, what are listeners doing when they listen to music in a focused manner?

One feature of focused listening is that it allows people to pay attention to the 'sounds themselves' – or perhaps, more specifically – to what it is that these sounds represent. There is some empirical evidence for the wide range of things that people hear in music: in a study in which British listeners were asked to describe what they heard when played extracts of music and everyday sounds, their answers varied enormously – as might be expected in response to such a broad question.[1] One characteristic that listeners mentioned was their perception of musical structures, such as rhythms, melodic contours, and textures. These elements of music have been the focus of the majority of research in music perception and cognition over the last thirty years, perhaps because they are the primary form-bearing features of Western music from the common practice era (approximately 1550–1900) which has been the musical genre on which most psychology of music research has concentrated. However, listeners were more likely to describe what the sounds meant to them, whether this was in terms of an extra-musical association, an affective quality, a physical space, or the source of the sound. This suggests a type of listening in which listeners hear 'beyond' the acoustic characteristics of the sound to the meanings that music has for them. The next two sections deal with these two conceptions of listening – structural and meaningful – in turn.

5.2 **Hearing musical structure**

Tariq turns on his radio and tunes in to his favourite classical music station. It is ten minutes into 'Exploring Music', and the urbane

---

[1] The categories of response that people gave included the physical source of the sound, genre, acoustic characteristics, emotion, function, social context, physical proximity of the listener to the sound, the physical space suggested by the sound, and the performance skill with which the music was executed (Dibben, 2001). Other accounts of this ecological approach to music perception can be found in the work of Eric Clarke (2005b), and Luke Windsor (2000).

voice of the programme's host is encouraging his listeners to hear the way in which the opening theme of the first movement of Mozart's popular C Major piano sonata (K. 545) consists of little more than a slightly embellished tonic arpeggio on the main beats of the bar, answered by a little scalar descent; and how that deceptively simple theme is then quickly dissolved into a sequence of faster scales that moves steadily downwards by step. 'A simple, even obvious, cadence brings the material to its conclusion', the radio host observes, 'to be followed by an innocent little trill right in the middle of the piano that expands from a semitone' (he plays it), 'to a whole tone' (plays again) 'and then a minor third – at which point superimposed above it, and in a more singing register of the piano, there appears the sonata's second theme – now in the dominant – G Major – of the sonata's original C. And what is this new theme that seems at first hearing so different from the first? None other than a slightly embellished inversion and rhythmic reversal of that same little opening arpeggio – but how changed it now sounds, elevated into a different register, pointing downwards rather than up, and flowing into a condensed sequential treatment. This is the beguiling beauty of Mozart's music: the apparently natural way in which it weaves together and unifies the motivic material in balanced phrases, and leads the listener on through its sure-footed tonal journey'.

A culturally dominant attitude, particularly in relation to classical music, is the idea that music is a form of sonic 'play' – a kind of acoustical chess, in which the aim of listening is to identify and follow the sequence of 'moves' and to take pleasure in appreciating the cleverly wrought structures. Music, from this perspective, is an autonomous art form, albeit with origins in socially embedded practical activities, such as seasonal festivals, religious rituals, social ceremonies, working practices, and so on, but which started to detach itself from such contexts and become increasingly structurally complex during the seventeenth and eighteenth centuries.[2] This development of 'function-lessness' is, perhaps paradoxically, regarded as one of the crowning achievements of Western art music. Having become free from everyday practical concerns, music could aspire to lofty ideals: it has become, for many people, a special realm of pure, abstracted, and particularly intense experience, with a spiritual or religious quality reflecting the universality of human concerns.[3]

If music is to be heard as an abstract narrative ('pure structure in time', as it has sometimes been portrayed) the listener must be able to identify and make sense of musical structures. However rarefied the eventual experience might be claimed to be, it has to start with the tangible attributes of musical sounds.[4] Acoustics (the physics of sound) has well-developed and sophisticated methods to describe and observe the physical characteristics and behaviour of sounds, expressed in terms of the amplitude (power), frequency (speed of oscillation), duration, and superimposition of waveforms, but this is very different from describing how they are perceived by human beings.

One striking finding made by music psychologists is that the physical and perceptual attributes of music are not identical. For example, although pitch (a psychological property in that it is the product of cognition) is related to the physical parameter of frequency (the number of times a waveform repeats within a second), the doubling of a frequency does not correspond to a 'doubling' of pitch.

---

[2] There has been debate about the history of this process, and the extent to which this progressive autonomy should be seen as real or illusory. See, for example, Lydia Goehr's (1992) book *The Imaginary Museum of Musical Works: An Essay in the Philosophy of Music*, and also the collection of essays in *The Musical Work: Reality or Invention* edited by Michael Talbot (2000).

[3] A fictional expression of this kind of attitude can be found in Hermann Hesse's (1943) novel *The Glassbead Game*.

[4] There are those who claim the virtues of the musical experience of silent score reading (e.g. the composer Brahms claimed that he found it superior to hearing live performance). This is a skill that is confined to a tiny proportion of humanity, however, and there must be some doubt about whether the claims for it are really anything more than a rather posturing kind of connoisseurship.

Furthermore, in many circumstances, pitch is perceived in terms of discrete categories of pitch classes, organized in terms of frequency *ratios* and repeated at octave intervals, rather than as points along a single linear continuum of frequencies. Similarly, although our perception of loudness increases as the amount of energy in the sound increases, it certainly does not do so in anything like a one-to-one relationship (for example, a doubling of energy corresponds to much less than a doubling of perceived loudness), and it also interacts with frequency and texture. And in the time domain rhythm, tempo, and perceived large-scale form all have complex and elusive relationships with the passage of physical (clock) time. Auditory perception is not a simple mirroring of external reality but is mediated by biological, perceptual and cultural factors.

Many studies have investigated listeners' abilities to hear the structures typically identified by standard music theory (SMT): for example, it has been found that appropriately enculturated listeners hear hierarchical relationships between discrete pitch categories (a fundamental component of SMT), contributing to the perception of stability and instability, a sense of the music's direction towards a musical goal, and allowing judgements of expressive performance as discussed in Chapter 3. To what extent listeners perceive the objects of SMT such as key relationships or large-scale hierarchical musical structures, or 'construct' them as they listen to music, is a question that continues to interest music psychologists and theorists alike.

Let us consider what might be involved in identifying and making sense of the kinds of musical structures and processes pointed out in Tariq's radio programme and which form the basis of this kind of 'purely musical' listening experience. In order to hear the music's opening theme as 'an embellished tonic arpeggio on the main beats of the bar', a listener would have to be sensitive to the tonality of the music (the sense of key), the presence and specific organization of its metrical structure (its pattern of beats), and the particular pattern of intervals (a major third followed by a minor third) that defines the tonic arpeggio in a major key. The terminology of this description (as for most of the rest of the imagined radio analysis) is couched in the language

of SMT, and the implication of this is that a sensitive and attentive list-
ner should be aware of the structures and processes described by this
terminology. A considerable amount of research has investigated the
psychological reality of these structures and processes, circling around
the question of whether these are simply convenient ways to *describe*
music from the perspective of SMT, or whether these are the kinds of
entities that people actually perceive.[5]

In broad terms, the outcome of this extensive body of research is to
show that SMT descriptions of music correspond rather closely with
what people can be shown to hear. Suitably enculturated listeners can
be shown to have a sense of the tonality and metre of the music within
a very short span of notes, and to be sensitive to feelings of tension and
relaxation as the music moves to more or less distant tonalities, or
becomes more or less rhythmically stable and unstable. They can identify conventional melodic archetypes, differentiate between variants of
a given melody, and spot specific melodic intervals. They can identify
some aspects of the larger-scale formal structure of complete pieces of
music (although questions have been raised about the perceptibility
of some aspects of larger-scale tonal structure), make judgements as to
where fragments of a piece belong in an overall design, and whether the
tempo of a performance seems appropriate for the music.[6] The kind of
description that Tariq's radio host provides, which might be characterized as a 'drama of structure', is therefore largely borne out as plausible
in terms of the skills required for listening to music, and although some
of these are significantly more developed in listeners who have had
formal musical training, many of them are similarly developed for
enculturated listeners who have not had formal training.

---

[5] Discussions of the relationship between music theory and the psychology of music, and
whether the psychology of music should be concerned with demonstrating the reality or
not of music theoretic entities, can be found in Cook (1994) and Cross (1998).

[6] As already mentioned, these findings are spread across a very large body of research that
constitutes the great bulk of the existing literature in the psychology of music. Useful surveys
(some more specialized, some more general) can be found in the following: Dowling and
Harwood (1985), Sloboda (1985), Krumhansl (1990), Temperley (2001), Huron (2006),
and *Grove Music Online* entry on 'Psychology of Music' (http://www.grovemusic.com).

These are important findings, and have raised further questions of great interest to psychologists about the nature of the mental structures and mechanisms that are responsible for these skills and sensitivities. How does a listener pick up enough information from just three or four notes – which are almost certainly not played with metronomic accuracy – to continue tapping in time with the music, or make a judgement about whether a subsequent note is on or off the beat? How does a listener perceive the pattern of a melody with enough precision and stability to distinguish between a variant that is a direct transposition and another that has a different pattern of intervals? How can a listener judge the sense of 'balance' between two phrases of music that may have very different numbers and kinds of events, but which perform equivalent functions in a formal design? How can a listener judge whether a harmonic shift is to a more or less remote region? How do listeners judge the importance of a structural division in a piece that they have only heard two or three times?

Many of these and similar questions have been answered using explanations based on the theory that listeners draw on hierarchical memory representations for music, or other types of mental models. In broad terms, psychologists believe that as people become more familiar with a particular genre of music – through so-called 'passive exposure', active listening, or explicit training – they develop internal representations, stored in long-term semantic memory,[7] which provide a hierarchically organized framework into which new sequences of events can be fitted. As long as the new events conform, in their specifics, to the general characteristics of material that is already familiar to the listener (in terms of their statistical distribution and the patterns of relationships between them), they will be organized and perceived in the same way. This process is clearly similar to that which occurs in language learning: once you are familiar with the structural regularities of a language and have some basic vocabulary, it is not hard to make sense

---

[7] For a more general discussion of human memory see Alan Baddeley's (1997) book *Human Memory: Theory and Practice,* and for musical memory specifically Bob Snyder's (2000) book *Music and Memory: An Introduction.*

of novel utterances as long as they broadly conform to what you already know. In order to understand how listeners make sense of music, therefore, it has been suggested that we must understand how they develop and draw on appropriate mental representations of music, or in other words how they build musical 'models'.

In some respects these models make use of specifically musical relationships and kinds of organization (such as the properties of tonality and metre, for example), but they also borrow extensively from more generic models of human perception and cognition. The analogy with language has already been mentioned, and in a similar fashion, melody perception may make use of general principles found in vision or speech (as proposed by Gestalt theories), and rhythm perception may make use of more general mechanisms of time and sequence perception.[8] It seems very likely, or even certain, that listening to music makes use of general perceptual mechanisms that are common to other aspects of auditory perception and memory, or even perception and memory as a whole – though the extent to which music perception should be regarded as a domain in its own right has also sparked controversy. In terms of recent debates between psychologists as to whether the mind is modular (a collection of special processors), or if it is non-modular, (a general-purpose device that adapts to different kinds of material[9]), the existence of a specific 'music module' has been proposed. Aniruddh Patel, for example, provides a wide-ranging discussion of the overlapping and non-overlapping properties of music and language based on neurophysiological evidence.[10]

---

[8] Jay Dowling and Dane Harwood, for example, are among many authors who discuss melody perception in terms of Gestalt principles (see their book *Music Cognition*). Dirk Jan Povel discusses rhythm perception in terms of more general theories of time and sequence processing e.g. Povel (1981); Povel and Essens (1985); for a rather different perspective, see Large and Jones (1999).

[9] See Fodor (1983). For a more recent review of the debate about modularity, see the paper by Barrett and Kurzban (2006).

[10] See Patel (2007).

The cognitive psychological approach to understanding the processes involved in listening to music has been adopted widely, but it presents some conceptual problems. Mental representations are psychological constructs – we can't see, hear or touch them. They have to be inferred from the results of perceptual experiments, which are often, necessarily, rather simplistic and may not reflect real-world listening. Furthermore it is not clear by what process mental representations are stored let alone organized into mental models, nor how listeners draw on them when they listen to music, either for the first time or on subsequent occasions. More generally, the cognitive psychological approach has been criticized for offering excessively abstract, static, and internalized explanations, divorced from any bodily response or physical action.

A consideration of musical listening raises the question of the extent to which music simply reflects, or attempts to expand, human perceptual and cognitive capacities. Greater understanding of human perceptual processes has led some researchers to highlight the disjunction that sometimes exists between the musical structures created by composers and improvisers, and heard musical structures.[11] For example, it has been claimed that the more complex attributes of serially composed or twelve-tone music simply cannot be perceived, and that whatever their compositional value, they play no part in the experience of listeners.[12] This is not to say that some compositional choices are more or less appropriate, since these are subject to the cultural contingencies of the time, but it does indicate that some strategies are less perceptually obvious than others.

---

[11] See, for example, the discussion in Fred Lerdahl's article "Cognitive Constraints on Compositional Systems" (1988).

[12] Twelve-tone serial music is music composed using various transformations of a specific ordering of all of the twelve chromatic semitones – a specific ordering that is usually fixed for the duration of a whole movement or piece. The theoretical claim made in Fred Lerdahl's (1988) 'Cognitive Constraints' article, already mentioned, is partially supported by empirical evidence provided by Krumhansl et al. (1987)

Another, related, line of enquiry involves the investigation of how cognitive constraints mediate compositional practices. One such piece of research has been undertaken by the US music psychologist David Huron, who has shown how experimentally established perceptual principles might account for the voice-leading characteristics of Western music of the common practice era, and even highlights aspects of voice-leading practice that have hitherto gone unnoticed.[13] This example illustrates how a complex and specific cultural activity such as music-making can be understood as the product of both deep-seated psychological constants and particular social and historical circumstances, and highlights the new insights that can be gained from taking a cognitive psychological approach.

5.3 **Hearing meanings**

Despite the prevalence of research into the perception of musical parameters, such as melodic contour, harmony, metre, rhythm, timbre, texture, and so on, there is evidence that listeners also experience music more holistically, in terms of its meanings. Two broad approaches dominate current musicological and philosophical theories of musical meaning. The first, in the tradition of formalist analysis of music, conceives of musical meaning in terms of musical structure. According to this view, musical meaning is primarily *musical*, and is tied to, even identical with, attributes of musical structure, so that analyses of this kind can sometimes give the impression that the writer has simply substituted expressive labels for technical ones. The second approach argues that musical meaning is a social construction. According to this view, the meanings that listeners derive from specific pieces have a more or less arbitrary relationship to their sonic characteristics, although these meanings may be stable within a particular cultural context. This latter approach is influenced by the linguistic theory of Ferdinand de Saussure, and is part of a semiotic tradition in musical analysis. In distinguishing between these two broad approaches a wide variety of

---

[13] See David Huron (2001).

theories of musical meaning have been summarized. However, it high-lights an as yet unresolved problem: how to understand meaning as both dependent on musical structure and culturally constructed. One way of avoiding this problem is to argue that music does not have to have a specific meaning but has the potential for particular meanings to emerge given particular circumstances.[14] This relates to the concept of affordance, which is central to ecological psychology (discussed in Chapter 2).

In order to understand affordance, it is helpful to return to the dis-tinction drawn earlier between hearing musical sounds and hearing meanings. According to the ecological view, environmental sounds – like all perceptual information – are important for our survival, and our perceptual systems have evolved to attend to what sounds afford for us as organisms. This means that in many circumstances, what a sound means for us will be more relevant than what it sounds like. Take the example of the sound of an approaching police siren: listening to this sound from playback equipment, a listener might pay attention to the change in dynamics and pitch as the vehicle approaches and then passes by the microphone (an instance of the Doppler effect[15]). But hearing this sound while trying to cross a busy road, a listener will be much more likely to take note of the sound's meaning (that there is a vehicle approaching, and its likely direction and speed), since to dwell on the quality of the sound in this context would be downright dangerous.

There is potentially a huge amount of information in the sounds people hear: the spatial location of sound sources (conveyed by time and phase differences between the two ears, and the 'shadowing' effects of the pinna – the outer ear); the speed of movement of a sound source (derived from the changes in intensity, pitch [Doppler effect], and

---

14 For a discussion of theories of musical meaning, and a model of how meaning is both dependent on musical structure and culturally conditioned, see Nicholas Cook (2001).

15 The 'Doppler effect' describes the change in pitch experienced when a moving sound source passes a stationary listener, or when a person moves quickly past a stationary sound source. The pitch rises as the listener and source approach one another, and then falls as they move apart, because the decreasing distance between the two compresses the wavelength and increases the effective frequency of the signal, whereas the increasing distance stretches the wavelength, and decreases the frequency.

signal-to-noise ratio of the source in relation to its surroundings); the size and mass of a sound source, and any force exerted on it, and so on. But what role do these kinds of information play in relation to music listening? The acoustic attributes of music are obviously an important component of listening, and listeners pay attention to the quality of timbre produced by a particular performer or ensemble. But one aspect of that sound is what it tells us about its source. For example, the listener may hear tension in a singer's vocal tract and interpret it as emotional intensity or anxiety. Similarly, an orchestral crescendo can be heard as merely an increase in dynamics, but it might also be understood by the listener as the sound of a large object approaching, as would be the case were the same acoustic change encountered in a 'real-world' (i.e. non-musical) context – ideas that are explored further in Chapter 6. In some kinds of music, the acoustic characteristics of sounds are transformed and combined with other sounds in a manner that encourages listeners to attend to their purely sonorous characteristics and the meanings that are thereby evoked, rather than focusing on their sources.

Whether listeners pay attention to the acoustic characteristics of the music or to its meanings depends on how they listen, and what they are listening *for* – defined not just by their preoccupations, but by cultural conventions, received knowledge about how to listen in particular circumstances, and the material characteristics of the listening situation. The attentive style of listening associated with listening to art music in concert halls, for instance, or listening to music on headphones at home, facilitates paying attention to the characteristics of the sounds themselves, and to their development and succession in time. Arguably, certain compositional styles lend themselves better than others to this mode of listening: for example, keeping track of the varied development of a short musical idea through a piece of music requires attentive listening, whereas unchanging and repetitive musical structures might be less rewarding to listen to in the same way, but much more satisfying to dance to. In either case, listeners' knowledge and intentions determine how they listen and thus, at least to some extent, what they hear. Yet sitting still and listening to music as the primary object of attention – what might be called focused listening – can be seen as the exception to everyday listening practices rather than the norm, and from that perspective looks like a rather peculiar activity.

Indeed, people do not only perceive and understand music when they deliberately attend to it: they dance, tap their feet, move in synchrony to certain aspects of musical structure, and respond to music in ways that suggest they have taken in and understood the music, even if it is not their main focus of attention. Unfortunately, research into the perception of music has less to say about the psychological processes by which music is assimilated in situations where it is background to some other task. Understanding the perception and cognition of music is most advanced in the context of deliberate and attentive listening, perhaps because it is assumed that other kinds of listening involve the same processes but simply capture less of the available information. Thus we are confronted with a paradox when it comes to thinking about the relationship between using and hearing music: despite evidence that focused listening is a relatively rare activity in comparison with other kinds of listening, and exemplifies an ideology that constructs the repertoire with which it is most commonly associated as a particularly 'functionless' form of music, it is the 'use' of this functionless music that has received most attention from researchers in the field of music perception and cognition.

Summary

Some ways of listening to music seem to demonstrate the functionlessness of music – its ability to represent nothing other than itself – yet psychological and sociological perspectives on listening suggest that music is far from autonomous, performing a range of functions for individuals and groups of listeners. Research on listening also reveals the differences between the physical characteristics of musical sound, and its psychological manifestations. These differences show how our perception of the musical world is shaped by the interaction of physical, biological, psychological, and cultural factors. It is tempting to think of the meanings people derive from musical experiences as entirely subjective and therefore unfathomable, yet from the perspective of ecological psychology such meanings are understood as the outcome of a reciprocal relationship between listeners with their preoccupations and capacities on the one hand, and music, including its acoustic characteristics, associated cultural conventions, and material characteristics of the listening situation on the other. The idea that music is autonomous elicits resistance to the notion that it can, or indeed should, be 'used', yet as this chapter has argued, there is evidence that music affords important individual and group uses. The next two chapters discuss some of these functions in more detail.

Chapter 6

Individuals using music

6.1 Enhancing human life

As well as being a father of three young children, and working as an electrician, Keith is a member of a Big Band. The band meets upstairs in a local pub every Tuesday evening for 2 hours and is currently rehearsing for a performance at a friend's wedding party. Keith tries to fit in at least two sessions of practice at home between the weekly rehearsals, and although he enjoys his participation in the band, it makes demands of him and the rest of his family: his absence on Tuesday evenings means that his partner stays at home to care for their children, he rehearses his part in his head during snatched moments at work, and puts aside other family and domestic commitments in order to attend the extra rehearsals needed nearer the time of the performance. On top of this, he buys copies of instrumental parts, concert clothes, and pays an annual subscription fee. On the day of the performance, the Big Band plays to a gathering of friends, family and other wedding guests. He is pleased with his playing on the night, and looks forward to learning the new pieces that they will perform later in the summer.

Engaging in musical and other kinds of recreational activities (such as games and sports) is one means by which people achieve personal fulfilment. Psychological research on why people find particular activities enjoyable and intrinsically rewarding has focused on the transitory states of optimal experience, sometimes termed 'self-actualization', 'peak' experience, or 'flow' that seem to be important in people's commitment to these pastimes.[1] Activities as diverse as rock climbing, dancing, composing, and basketball have been investigated; yet qualitative research shows that some activities (e.g. music and sex) enable the experience of 'flow' more successfully than others. An explanation for this can be found by analysing the specific characteristics of flow, and comparing these to the musical activities of performing, composing, and listening.

First, activities which tend to be experienced in a state of flow encourage a narrowing of the field of attention and allow people to ignore distractions and focus their actions so that they feel in control of their environment: for instance, a composer manipulates musical materials, creating a musical sound-world, a performer controls the production of sound, which blocks out other auditory distractions and focuses attention. Second, flow activities offer continuous feedback, including auditory and kinaesthetic feedback in the case of playing a musical instrument. Such activities involve an ongoing match between challenge and skill in which the challenge presented increases as an individual's skills increase – with the consequence that people feel that they never cease to find opportunities to 'learn new things'. The challenges vary to such a degree in music, which involves different contexts, performance styles, repertoires, and levels of technical difficulty, that there will always be limitless opportunities for expert as well as novice performers to match their skills. Third, attention is often more focused and feedback on skills more valuable when the activity being undertaken is perceived as dangerous or risky. So, for example, giving a less than satisfactory public performance is potentially risky to the musician's self-esteem, but can focus his or her attention on the need to prepare adequately, and provide useful feedback on progress.

The outcomes of a musical activity (a musical performance, a composition) are often cited by the individuals concerned as justifications

---

[1] 'Self-actualization' and 'peak experience' are discussed at length by Abraham Maslow in his books *Toward a Psychology of Being* (1968) and *The Farther Reaches of Human Nature* (1976). The concept of 'flow' was originated by Mihály Csikszentmihályi, and is set out in his books *Beyond Boredom and Anxiety* (1975) and *Flow: The Psychology of Optimal Experience* (1990). An overview of strong experiences with music is given by Alf Gabrielsson (2001) in his chapter 'Emotions in strong experiences with music'.

for the activity. However, Keith doesn't stop playing in the band because the performance is over: the outcome is useful as a goal to work towards and a way to measure his development, but it is the flow experience itself that provides the motivation for his sustained engagement. Yet in the case of musical and other artistic endeavours, outcomes such as performances and art objects can in turn trigger peak experiences in audience members; so, for example, the people at Keith's perform-ance may experience strong emotional reactions to the music he plays. The next section considers how and why music is experienced as expressing and inducing emotions, and how music can influence affec-tive life.

6.2 **Music and affect**

6.2.1 **Emotion and music**

Anna is painting the walls of the living room in her house, listening to the radio as she works. Suddenly, she's aware of the ascending harp arpeggiation, warm sustained string sound, and melody of the aria 'O Mio Babbino Caro' ('Oh My Beloved Father') from Puccini's opera *Gianni Schicchi* and feels a shiver down her spine. The song has great significance for her due to its associations with her father who died recently. She stops painting and listens. As she listens, she's aware of the intensity of the singer's voice – the arching melody reaching high into the soprano's register, the flow of vocal energy sustained across the long notes which end each phrase – and feels the hair on the back of her neck stand on end as the singer's voice soars the octave jump each time to the high A. She feels the music gather-ing pace and energy as the opening melody repeats the first two phrases, but pushes on into the high register in an extension of the previous melodic lines. The vocal line is taken up by the strings as the voice falls silent (*vorrei morir* – 'I want to die'), and the return of the voice in the following phrase is hesitant and pleading: each phrase stated separately this time, the second without the octave leap and all the more poignant for it. She finds the lyrics most profound at the end – the moment when, as she puts it, she 'feels it most intensely'.

Music is an important source of, and accompaniment to, emotional experience for many people. When people talk about emotion in every-day conversation, they generally refer to a relatively transient feeling state using an adjective, such as 'happy', 'angry', or 'sad', which has been evoked by an event which has personal significance for them. Yet this feeling state is just one component of an emotional reaction. For example, Anna's intense emotional reaction involves not only a feeling state but memories of her father, her thoughts about those memories and what they mean for her at that moment, a strong physical response (a shiver down the spine, hair standing up on the back of the neck), and a change in her behaviour (she stops painting and devotes her attention to the music). Thus, from a psychological perspective, an emotion is a complex response to an event of personal significance, involving cognitive appraisal, physiological changes, and motor processes taking the form of behavioural changes.

Emotions guide our actions, enable expression of our states to others, and allow us to interpret other people. Emotional responses to every-day events are useful for survival, especially where we may have inadequate information about a situation, or conflicting goals. Imagine you are walking down a road and a large dog suddenly jumps out at you barking aggressively: you feel your skin temperature rise and your breathing and heartbeat quicken. These physical sensations are symptoms of the so-called 'fight or flight' response. This increase in rate of respiration and faster heartbeat enables the muscles of the limbs to be supplied with the oxygen necessary to prepare them for action in a potentially dangerous situation. These changes happen in an instant, before you have had time to realize that the barking is excitement and friendliness rather than threatening aggression, because parts of the emotional response system have evolved to respond before a situation has been appraised fully. In this way, humans gain the best possible chance of survival, even though the physiological component of our emotions is activated by what can turn out to be false alarms.

One major difference between emotions in everyday life and emotional reactions to music is that music does not appear to have the same consequences for survival. This therefore raises questions about the mechanisms by which music affords emotional experiences. An important distinction implicit in Anna's experience described above, is that between the emotions represented by music (here, the emotions attributed to the female character, Lauretta, played by the soprano), and those experienced by the listener (Anna's own affective experience as she listens to the aria). In this example there is a close correspondence between the two, because Anna partly identifies her own personal experiences with the narrative of the operatic aria, but this is not necessarily always the case. The extent to which the two are really separable is a matter of debate, but the distinction does suggest that the mechanisms by which music represents or elicits emotions may differ, as may the kinds of emotion involved.

It is possible to identify six main mechanisms of emotion induction and representation.[2] First, from a psychological perspective music is auditory information, and as such gives rise to emotional responses because sounds signal information important to human survival. As we saw in Chapter 5, sounds specify the type, spatial location, and size of their sources, and it is therefore likely that many of their perceptual properties influence the meanings that music has for listeners, and their emotional reactions to it. A loud sound, for example, can specify a large source or a source very close to the listener, and an increase in dynamic level, such as an orchestral crescendo, specifies either an object approaching, or movement towards an object. In the acoustic environment, both large and/or approaching objects represent potential threats and are therefore likely to elicit orienting responses such as turning the body so as to perceive or respond to them better. If the emotional response system is to offer sufficient protection, it is unlikely to 'switch off' in the presence of events that in truth do not require 'flight or fight', since it needs to err on the side of false alarm activation. Thus, as a form of auditory information, music is just as likely to elicit emotional responses as any other kind of environmental event.

---

[2] Patrik Juslin provides a useful overview of processes of emotion induction in 'Emotional responses to music' in *The Oxford Handbook of Music Psychology* (2009) from which five of these six mechanisms are drawn (the exception being semantic meaning).

Even at a more fine-grained level, sounds convey information about their sound sources that may contribute to affective experience. For example, in the aria described above, the singer's vocal timbre conveys information about the singer's size, age, physical, and psychological state. In practice these (potential) vocal cues may be inaudible to most listeners, or be stylized to such an extent – as in much opera singing – that they are considerably reduced in salience. Nonetheless, the physical characteristics of vocal and indeed instrumental production (e.g. the sound of a violinist's bow, the breathing of a wind player, the squeak of a guitarist's left hand on the strings) are an inevitable component of performance and hence may play a part in eliciting listeners' emotional reactions.

A second related route by which music may afford affective experience is through emotional contagion, in which the listener perceives the performer's emotion and 'mimics' this expression internally. It may be that hearing 'sorrow' in someone else's musical, vocal, or gestural expression causes the listener to take on some of those same characteristics in a mirroring of the expressive conditions.

The third and fourth routes by which music may elicit or represent emotion are evaluative conditioning, and episodic memory. In evaluative conditioning, an emotion may be induced because the music often occurred at the same time as another positive or negative event, such that when the positive or negative event itself is later absent, the music nonetheless evokes the same emotional reaction. In the case of episodic memory, music may evoke a memory of an event from the listener's life such that when the memory is evoked, so too is an emotional reaction to that memory. One explanation of Anna's emotional response when she heard the aria is that it elicited an association between the music and former times, perhaps because it was a piece her father often played when they spent time together (evaluative conditioning). Or perhaps, Anna recalled a particular occasion on which the music was played and reacted as much to the memory of her father as the music itself (episodic memory). Indeed, the attempt to separate the music from the memory may be impossible, since they are so bound up with one another.

Fifth, whole pieces of music, or musical materials, may come to be associated with specific meanings perhaps due to their history of use – a form of semantic meaning. Some writers on emotion and music have tried to identify the specific meanings of certain musical materials, such as particular melodic intervals, or combinations of melodic, harmonic, timbral, and rhythmic features.[3] Particular musical materials may become associated with specific meanings either because practical factors make certain materials more or less likely to be used in conjunction with particular meanings, such as the loud dynamic of brass instruments making them suitable for outdoor activities; or because there is an iconic resemblance between musical materials and extra-musical phenomena, such as that between deliberately distorted electric guitar sounds and the signification of power. The stability of these associations is largely dependent upon the consistency with which materials have been used by musicians and the listener's familiarity with the style.

Some research suggests that the meanings afforded by musical materials may have considerable cross-cultural commonality. For instance, in one study, listeners unfamiliar with the Hindustani rasa-raga system perceived some of the same emotional expression in extracts of that music as did expert listeners, because the same psychophysical cues are associated with the same broad categories of emotion in each culture: joy and anger are both associated with fast tempi, for example, whereas sadness and peacefulness are associated with slow tempi.[4] When it comes to the expression of emotions, however, different cultures may use the same parameters in similar ways but the emotions themselves

---

[3] For example, brass instruments have historically been used by the military, such that for enculturated listeners they have acquired an association with hunting and an aggressive and heroic type of masculinity. This association remains salient today, as in the themes and orchestration of music for the *James Bond* films in which the prominent brass instrumentation of the theme tune contributes to the macho image of the James Bond character. For two different approaches to the meaning associated with musical materials, see Philip Tagg and Bob Clarida's (2003) *Ten Little Title Tunes: Towards a Musicology of the Mass Media*, and Deryck Cooke's (1959) book *The Language of Music*.

[4] This study is reported in Balkwill and Thompson (1999).

(their causes, the way they are framed and appraised, associated behaviour and regulation) have been shown to differ cross-culturally, along with the values and worldviews held by people of different cultures. So, for example, Japanese beliefs about modesty require that the self remains inconspicuous, and so *haji* (the emotion elicited by behaviour which is immodest) is more prominent in Japanese than British life.[5] So although there may be systematic relationships between musical parameters and the general characteristics of emotions, such as their degree of energy or valence (i.e. positivity or negativity), universals are unlikely to offer a complete explanation of the expression of emotion in music.

A sixth route by which music may represent or induce emotion, discussed in Chapter 3 in relation to expressive performance, is that music is experienced in terms of expectations for musical continuations and that when resolution of these musical expectations is delayed or thwarted, an arousal response is stimulated and listeners experience an emotional reaction.[6] These musical expectations arise due to basic grouping processes (Gestalt principles, for instance) and exposure to the commonalities of a style. Some evidence for the specific role of musical structures in emotional experience has been found in studies of Western classical music listening: analysis of the musical moments at which listeners had in the past experienced a strong physical–emotional reaction (sometimes termed 'chills and thrills') showed that many of the musical structures gave rise to clear expectations for musical continuation which were thwarted or delayed.[7] Anna's most intense physical response to 'O Mio Babbino Caro' occurs during bars 17 and 18 of the aria (Fig. 6.1). Part of the music's effect for Anna at this moment arises from the lyrics, and from the heightened state implied by the

---

[5] Reviews of the debates surrounding the cross-cultural study of emotion can be found in Lutz and White (1986) and Mesquita and Frijda (1992).

[6] A detailed and sophisticated account of the role of expectation in emotional responses to music is given by David Huron in his book Sweet Anticipation: Music and the Psychology of Expectation (2006).

[7] John Sloboda's (1991) empirical investigation of emotional responses to structural expectations explores theories proposed previously by Leonard B. Meyer and George Mandler.

Fig. 6.1 Extract of 'O Mio Babbino Caro' from Puccini's *Gianni Schicchi*.

high tessitura of the soprano's voice at the moment Lauretta (the soprano's character) declares that if she is not to marry she would prefer to die ('*O Dio, vorrei morrir!*'). However, the theory of musical expectation also explains why this moment in particular should be associated with a heightened physical reaction. One notable feature of this place in the aria is its contravention of the sectional divisions set up earlier in the music: bar 17 is the moment when the expectation for sectional closure is thwarted by a four bar extension to the section. In the shorter term, the varied repetition of the descending melodic motif starting on the high A in bar 18 also blocks the expectation that the melody will descend from bar 17, as the immediately preceding phrase did. From a psychological perspective, these deviations from the norm for this aria play an orienting function, drawing the listener's attention to the music, and the physiological correlate of this orienting response is heightened arousal, potentially experienced as physiological responses such as a racing heart, shivers, goose bumps, and so on.

As noted in Chapter 3, in relation to performance expression, one problem with a theory of emotional response based upon expectations is that it seems to suggest that listeners should not experience an emotional reaction to music with which they are very familiar, since it holds no 'surprises' for them. Yet this is manifestly not the case: people often have strong emotional responses despite being very familiar with the music. This is partly because processing mechanisms continue to give rise to schematic (generalized) expectations even when an experienced listener has a veridical (specific) memory for a particular piece as a consequence of previous hearings.

The theory of musical expectancy also offers a possible explanation for the ineffability of emotional experience – the fact that music is often reported as having the shape of emotional experience, but as lacking the specificity and semantic content associated with emotions in daily life.[8] From a psychological perspective this experience of the form of an emotion without its content, is akin to experience of the physiological component of an emotion minus the element of cognitive appraisal. Research into the physiology of emotional experiences suggests that people sometimes experience emotional feelings without the cognitive component, giving rise to something like an emotional experience, and this may be what is happening in the case of emotional reactions to music. People who are injected with an arousal-inducing drug (such as epinephrine) but who are led to believe that the drug is unrelated to any physical effects they subsequently experience, report feeling 'as-if' they are angry/happy/sad and so on. They experience some of the physical sensations that would normally accompany these emotions, yet because these reactions have no identifiable cause (for them), they are not experienced as 'real' emotions.[9] In the case of music it may be that arousal due to structural expectancies has the form, but not the semantic content, of a complete emotional experience.

---

[8] Researchers who have discussed music's emotional character in terms of its flow of tensions and relaxations include Susanne Langer (1951) and Leonard B. Meyer (1956).

[9] For a discussion of the physiology of emotion and how emotional responses to music are influenced by body state see Dibben (2004).

This theory of musical expectations also explains why individuals report experiencing an intense emotional reaction at the same place in a particular piece of music, even though they may give widely divergent interpretations of the meaning of that moment for them. A combination of semantic contexts surrounding music (programme notes, lyrics, visual imagery), autobiographical associations with certain pieces or musical materials, and culturally shared patterns of association which may be more or less familiar and salient for different listeners, means that musical structures can provide a source for emotional experience with music, but the content of that experience is largely dependent on individual and situational factors. This lack of specificity (what Ian Cross has called 'floating intentionality'[10]) may paradoxically be music's strength as a means of communication, since it affords the experience of shared purpose between individuals or groups even when there may be disagreements.

The plurality of mechanisms by which music affords affective experience, and the diversity of sources the listener can draw upon in making sense of their experience, may account for the richness and apparent ineffability of affective experience with music. It also highlights the complexity of the task involved in understanding emotional experiences with music.

6.2.2 Mood regulation using music

Of the many different ways in which people use music in contemporary industrialized societies, one of the commonest is to regulate mood. Chapter 2 discussed how infant-directed speech is important for the co-regulation of emotion between infant and carer, as well as enabling infants to acquire prosodic and phonemic abilities, and to develop skills in social interaction. A survey of how Americans regulate their mood state carried out by Robert Thayer and others revealed that music is the third most popular means to get out of a bad mood, the third most

---

[10] For an overview of music's communicative ability from the perspective of evolution see Ian Cross 'The nature of music and its evolution' in *The Oxford Handbook of Music Psychology* 2009.

popular way to reduce tension and anxiety, and a popular way to raise energy levels (although less popular than sleeping, taking a shower, getting some fresh air, and drinking coffee).[11] Indeed, the notion that music is a form of entertainment is tantamount to saying that music is a means for people to alter their mood: to be entertained is to be pleasurably stimulated, and mood can be understood as a state of arousal (energy) with a particular valence (positive or negative). Many common uses of music can be understood as stemming from a desire either to change one's own mood, or that of other people. For example, common reasons that people cite for listening to music include making themselves feel better (or just different), and helping to attune themselves to a concurrent or anticipated activity – which might mean both physically in terms of achieving a desired state of alertness and arousal, and psychologically in terms of a desired emotional state.

The ability to manage moods is extremely important for effective psychological functioning since mood influences memory, decision-making, and evaluative judgements. People often employ strategies, consciously or unconsciously, for managing their mood states. Some of the complexities of mood management have emerged in experimental studies that track behaviour after people have been induced into a particular mood state. Typically, music is used to induce mood in these experimental studies, which is a drawback for research into music's effects on mood because researchers are less experienced with other mood induction methods. Experiments investigating the music people listen to after they have been induced into a particular mood state reveal different strategies for mood regulation: for example, whereas some people choose music which facilitates rumination on a negative emotion, others choose music which enables them to change a negative mood to a more positive one.[12] These studies have

---

[11] This research has been reported in Thayer et al. (1994). Other psychological studies of music and mood regulation in the everyday life of British and American adults include DeNora (2000), Sloboda et al. (2001), Stratton and Zalanowski (2003) and North et al. (2004).

[12] See Knobloch and Zillman (2002).

also shown that mood regulation is not simply a matter of trying to achieve an optimally positive mood and is dependent upon the needs of the individual at particular times, his or her personality traits, and the context. For example, studies of European and American men and women have found that women are far more likely than men to select music that will help them ruminate, reflecting a cultural tendency for women to blame themselves, and are more likely to distract themselves from an angry mood state, because in Western cultures it is less socially acceptable for women to express and feel anger. People are also much less likely to choose to ruminate when they think that they are going to have to meet and work with someone else on a common task shortly afterwards. So the decision to listen to music, and the particular music chosen, may both be a product of a desire to regulate a mood state, but the variability across people and situations means that there is no single musical prescription for a particular mood state.

In contemporary industrialized societies, music is most often listened to in the context of some other concurrent activity, and this can be attributed not only to the availability of digital and mobile listening technologies but also music's ability to influence mood.[13] For example, music is used by people in a range of work settings, including surgeons in operating theatres, air traffic controllers, and magazine editors. People cite a variety of reasons for using music in the workplace, most commonly to improve concentration on a task by blocking out noise and other distractions, to provide enough stimulation to avoid boredom (particularly during repetitive tasks), as well as to improve their mood (which arguably includes levels of arousal/stimulation), reduce stress and increase relaxation. Stress at work is one of the leading causes of ill-health and absence from work in industrialized nations. Furthermore, a

---

[13] For studies of mobile listening technologies, see Bull (2000, 2007). An entertaining history of muzak is given by Joseph Lanza in his book *Elevator Music: A Surreal History of Muzak, Easy-listening and Other Moodsong* (2004). Studies of the effects of music on work productivity and well-being include Lesiuk (2005) and Oldham et al. (1995).

dominant marketing strategy in the United Kingdom currently sells music in terms of its 'therapeutic' value to these potential consumers: for example, 'Drive Time' radio programming is marketed as a way to achieve a calm but energized state during commuting hours. A more informed understanding of current workplace listening practices, and their implications for well-being, could be useful for those wishing to provide music appropriate to particular needs, and for consumers who would then have an informed basis from which to judge the claims made by music providers regarding the benefits of their music.

6.3 Enhancing the cognitive skills and task performance of individuals

Many of the uses to which music is put are aimed at enhancing performance in some other activity: music while doing housework, driving, homework. But what is it that enables music to enhance these other activities? And is music ever detrimental to the things we may be trying to do at the same time?

6.3.1 Enhancing cognitive performance

There is a widely held belief in the West that involvement in classical music at an early age (and it is usually only classical music for which this assertion is made) can enhance general human development, symptomatic of which are the popularity of music classes for infants, which claim to improve general development alongside specifically musical skills, and the prevalence of recorded compilations of music that profess to boost children's learning. The claim that music can enhance non-musical aspects of development has also been used to justify the inclusion of music within school curricula and to support public funding of the arts.

Perhaps the most prominent claim of this sort is the idea that listening to music can enhance visuospatial skills – skills that are required for tasks as varied as driving, dress-making, and dry-stone walling. The scientific basis for these claims arises from experiments conducted into the effects of listening to music on a subsequent non-musical test.

Believing in research that seemed to show the power of classical music to enhance infant intelligence, the then governor of the State of Georgia, USA – Zell Miller – arranged for the parents of all newborn babies in Georgia to be issued with a free CD compilation of classical music – *Build Your Baby's Brain* (Sony, 1998). The music comprised movements and arias from works by popular classical composers, including Mozart, Bach, Beethoven, and Handel. The cover of the CD showed a collage of cute, ethnically mixed babies smiling out at the viewer, with musical notation superimposed, and the tagline (following on from *Build Your Baby's Brain*) 'Through the Power of Music'.

In the first experiment of this kind, American college students who listened for ten minutes to the first movement of Mozart's Sonata for Two Pianos in D major, K. 448, performed better on a visuospatial test carried out within ten minutes of listening to the music than they did after listening to a relaxation tape, or a period of silence. This finding was originally dubbed the 'Mozart Effect' (now, also a trademark for a set of recordings and products) but has since been generalized to include a range of other phenomena, including the reduction of epileptiform activity while listening to music for people who experience seizures,[14] improvements in cognitive and other abilities associated with keyboard lessons, improved classroom behaviour with background music, and stimulation of infant learning.[15]

The authors of the original study claimed that Mozart's music activates neurons used for spatial tasks, thereby leading to short-term improvements in visuospatial task performance[16]. However, this

---

[14] There are also some people for whom epilepsy is induced by music, as documented by Oliver Sacks in his book *Musicophilia: Tales of Music and the Brain* (2007).

[15] The classic study of the 'Mozart Effect' is by Rauscher et al. (1993). For a review of the many different studies of the 'Mozart Effect', see Hetland (2000).

[16] See also Suda et al. (2008).

research has proved extremely controversial, not least because of the many failures to replicate the results of the original study and criticisms of the speculative character of the particular model of the cortex on which the theory is based. Thus, as well as doubts about the reliability of the effect, there is disagreement as to what accounts for any cognitive or behavioural enhancements observed.

argument

An alternative explanation posits that any improvement in visuospatial skills is due to a combination of increased arousal, positive mood state, and preference for the stimuli.[17] Listening to music may elevate performance on cognitive tasks relative to other stimuli because it produces an optimal level of adrenalin in the brain, causing high arousal (low levels of adrenalin are associated with poor performance on a range of tasks). Yet, not all studies have found a correlation between arousal and performance, nor are all cognitive tasks improved, as would be predicted by this theory. Mood is also unable to provide a clear explanation for enhanced performance: there is empirical evidence that strong positive moods heighten arousal and thereby improve performance, but no corresponding evidence that strong negative emotions also enhance performance – as they should if enhancement is simply due to arousal.

Proponents of the beneficial effects of music on cognitive abilities point to the correlation between musical training and performance in non-musical school subjects, which implies a longer-term benefit than that found in the studies of visuospatial ability after listening to music. One study to have investigated this compared the cognitive abilities of two groups of children over a three-year period:[18] children receiving piano lessons obtained higher spatial ability scores than a

---

[17] See empirical work reported by Husain et al. (2002).

[18] A classic study showing longer-term effects of musical instruction on children's development is by Costa-Giomi (1999). Small one-day enhancements of spatioltemporal reasoning have also been found in children receiving piano lessons (Rauscher et al. 1997).

control group after one or two years of study, but there was no difference after three years. This short-term advantage which musical activities seem to confer suggests a range of other possible causes: the spatial arrangement of pitches on the keyboard, or the more abstract conceptualization of tonal pitch space may exercise visuospatial abilities, but equally improvements may be the consequence of one-to-one attention from an adult, a sense of mastery, or the discipline of practice, all of which may enhance self-esteem, confidence and patterns of learning.

Regardless of music's effects on specific cognitive abilities, numerous studies of the arts in education have concluded that music has benefits for personal development and social skills: different kinds of engagement in music can enhance awareness of others (through musical performance, and group composition), self-confidence (through the ability to perform in front of others), physical coordination and self-discipline (through instrumental practice).[19]

Thus, while music can help children develop their capabilities, this needs to be put in the context of wider developmental factors. The certainty with which some claims for music's beneficial effects on intellectual development have been taken up reflects a misplaced belief in, and misapplication of, a single high-profile study amplified by the easy fit between some of the available evidence and widespread beliefs about Western classical music: namely, its cultural prestige, an association between artistic skills and notions of musical 'genius', and a historical association between music and mathematics. The quick-fix solution which the 'Mozart Effect' seems to offer can't protect children from the disadvantages of poverty or dangerous environments and may even divert attention and resources away from other interventions that can.

---

[19] For a summary of the benefits of music within a wider educational context, see Harland et al. (2000).

6.3.2 **Music and concurrent tasks: Attention and distraction**

> It's Friday evening, and Heiner is driving home on the motorway. He was listening to the news and traffic reports as he wound his way to the motorway, but now he's feeling bored. The route is too familiar and the thought of the next two hours stuck in the car makes him impatient to be home. He sees that the traffic is flowing freely and switches to CD: a Frank Sinatra song starts playing and within a few minutes he's singing along. Occasionally, he notices that his speed is creeping up and he takes his foot off the accelerator. Ten minutes later the brake lights of the vehicles in front come on and the traffic in his lane slows to a halt. He stops singing and steps on the brakes. The traffic speeds up again, only to slow again a few minutes later, and he has to adjust his speed continuously. He turns off the music until there is a clear stretch of road.

Given that music appears to enhance physical and mental skills, are there circumstances under which music is ever detrimental to performance? One domain in which this is of considerable significance is music's potentially detrimental effects on the ability to drive safely. Anecdotal evidence suggests an association between loud, fast music and reckless driving, but how might music's ability to influence driving in this way be explained?

One possibility is that drivers entrain to temporal regularities in music, and that their speed (and aggression) is influenced accordingly. In other words, just as faster music tends to cause people to move around a store faster and to eat and drink faster so it causes people to drive at faster speeds, as they engage mentally and physically with ongoing repeated structures in the music. However, unlike the other instances where this effect has been demonstrated, driving does not involve the kinds of regular physical movement that might entrain to a musical pulse. It may be, then, that music influences the driver's state of arousal, which in turn influences mood and behaviour.

A second possibility is that music distracts drivers. Paradoxically, the reason why music is so popular while driving is also the reason why it can be detrimental to driving abilities: listening to music while driving helps alleviate boredom because it causes physiological arousal and elicits a degree of cognitive engagement (anticipating musical events in the piece, remembering situations where the music has been heard before, responding emotionally, understanding the lyrics, and so on). Music's ability to distract people from other sources of information competing for their attention explains its use in settings where it is important to take attention away from other events. For example, music may distract people from the discomfort they experience during exercise, allowing them to work harder and longer, perhaps because it reduces focus on the self.

However, music's ability to stimulate and distract can be problematic. Like many drivers, Heiner turns the music off when the driving situation becomes more demanding; drivers often turn music off when it is louder, faster, less familiar, or less well liked, or when the driving situation becomes more complex, because these attributes draw on the driver's (limited) attentional resources. Drivers may be twice as likely to make a poor driving decision or have an accident when they listen to fast (120 bpm) as opposed to slow (60 bpm) music, and reaction times are decreased by as much as 20% in the context of loud music (95 db).[20] However, individuals differ with regard to the level of arousal optimal to task performance, so that the dynamic level and tempo of music found arousing by one person will be distracting for another. These individual differences, and the constantly changing demands of the driving situation, make it impossible to specify with any degree of exactness 'safe' driving music, much as insurance companies and music providers would find it profitable to do so. However, one survey of the listening habits of British drivers and their safety record (derived from evidence of 'no claims' on their vehicle insurance, and self-reported

---

[20] These findings are reported in Brodsky (2002) and BBC News (2004a).

accident history) suggests that those drivers who do not listen to music while driving tend to be the safest.[21]

Summary

As this chapter illustrates, psychological research into music has much to say about individual experience and behaviour. Music is one means by which people enhance the quality of their life, achieving peak experiences of great intensity and personal significance, experiencing the absorption of flow states, and attaining self-actualization. Within many cultures, music is valued for its ability to express and induce emotional experiences. Cross-cultural studies of music reveal the different ways in which music is conceptualized in relation to people's emotional lives, and highlights the extent to which, certainly within contemporary Western culture, music is understood, and used, as a tool for the regulation of affect. Cross-cultural studies also highlight the extent to which what we think of as a commonsensical relationship with music, with a taken-for-granted place in everyday life, can be understood as the product of particular economic and social conditions, in which music is a product which can be put to instrumentalist uses (i.e. as a 'solution' for the 'problems' of the twenty-first century individual). The force of culture is therefore strong in shaping music's relationship with affect, despite evidence for significant similarities in the ways in which emotion in music is expressed and perceived across cultures that arise from biological commonality and shared ecological responses to environmental events. In this latter respect, the relationship between human and animal non-verbal communication, and the evolutionary origin of this capacity, has considerable potential for our understanding of musical meaning and communication.[22] This chapter has also given some examples of the ways in which music can enhance, and also

---

[21] See Dibben and Williamson (2007).

[22] See the collection of essays in *Human Communicative Musicality*, edited by Stephen Malloch and Colwyn Trevarthen (2008).

detract from cognitive skills and the performance of concurrent tasks. The instrumentalist focus on music is once again evident in the extent to which some findings, such as the claims of short-term improvement in spatial reasoning associated with listening to certain music, can quickly become transformed into misleading popular myths.

Chapter 7

Groups using music

7.1 Collective action and group cohesion

7.1.1 Structuring time, synchronizing body movements, and pacing work

In one way or another, all musical traditions combine music and movement, either through the direct associations such as dancing and the movements of performers, or less overt movements such as foot tapping or body swaying exhibited by listeners in musical traditions that suppress dancing, such as Western concert music. One view is that music's ability to induce a sense of movement is purely symbolic or metaphorical, but an alternative is that the sense of movement comes about through hearing in sound the movements of the performers, so that music creates a direct sense of virtual movement.

Metrical and rhythmic structures are important aspects of the temporal structure of music, to which movement and dance relate. From a psychological perspective, metre (a hierarchy of strong and weak beats) enables the listener to anticipate regularly occurring events in the auditory environment; while rhythms are specific patterns of events, which may or may not be regular, and are nested within larger metrical structures. In order to anticipate events, it is necessary to have some form of time-keeper, and two main theories of time-keeping have been proposed: clock models of time perception suggest that listeners encode the time intervals between beats; oscillator models propose a system of attentional peaks in which expectation is tuned to periodicities in the music.[1]

---

[1] For an overview of different models of time perception, and a theory of metre and rhythm perception, see Justin London's *Hearing in Time: Psychological Aspects of Musical Meter* (2004).

What makes the perception of time and rhythm particularly fascinating is that, unlike pitch for instance, humans do not have an organ dedicated to the perception of time.

As illustrated at the beginning of this book by reference to Diana's funeral (see Chapter 1), music's ability to structure time is exploited in ritual and ceremonial contexts. For example, a conventional Church of England wedding includes music to process to at beginning and end, the singing of hymns (in collective worship), and sometimes music played during the signing of the register. Each of these components has its own particular social function, and together, they provide a means of structuring the occasion. In other contexts, music is employed in circumstances involving changed states of consciousness. It is often claimed that music is a way of triggering trance states in ritual contexts, although it may be the case, rather, that music provides a structure and social context within which trance states can take place.[2]

At a more local level, music is a useful means for synchronizing and pacing other kinds of activities. The creation of pulse in music (a repeating, periodic accent), and the regular organization of the pulse into characteristic patterns of twos and threes, facilitates accurate motor coordination, allowing people to anticipate and place in time the physical movements needed to perform a task with precision and efficiency. Hence, music's ability to structure time makes it particularly useful in collective work where it helps coordinate and synchronize the movements of a group of people engaged in performing a common task.

Indeed, many forms of music bear traces of their origin in specific forms of collective physical labour. The structure of British sea shanties matches the tasks each would have been sung to: so, for instance, a song comprising alternating solo and chorus, such as 'Blow the Man Down', would have been sung during intermittent tasks such as hauling sails, whereas songs with longer verse and chorus ('A-rovin'' and 'Shenandoah')

---

[2] For different accounts of how music socializes or triggers trance states, see Gilbert Rouget's *Music and Trance: A Theory of the Relations between Music and Possession* (1985) and Judith Becker's *Deep Listeners: Music, Emotion and Trancing* (2004).

were used for more continuous tasks, such as operating the capstan or windlass.[3] Another example, this time used to pace the work of a single person, are the melodies of the Ma river songs from Thanh Hoa province in Vietnam, which are named according to the different stages in the journey of a rowing boat, and whose melodies are accompanied by the pounding rhythms of the feet on the planks of the boat. In all these cases, typical of work-music, the structuring of time, the pacing, the synchronization, and the coordination of physical movements are provided by an appropriate pulse, phrase structure, and larger-scale form. Similar characteristics underlie the uses of recorded music in workplaces, epitomized by music providers such as the Muzak Corporation – although here workers are listeners rather than performers, and are subject to a pace set for them by the recording, rather than being self-generated. There is some evidence that worker productivity is directly related to musical tempo, particularly when tasks are mundane and repetitive.

That music can sometimes unwittingly influence movements is evident from research into the effects of music on consumer behaviour. Music can influence purchasing by changing the speed of movement inside a store and therefore the amount of time spent shopping. The speed at which people walk around a store tends to increase or decrease with the tempo of background music: moderately paced music (less than about 70 bpm) encourages consumers to spend more time (and more money) than faster music. Similarly, the speed at which people eat and drink increases with the tempo of music.[4] The choice of music played in restaurants, bars, and stores can therefore be used to manipulate customers' length of stay and how much they are likely to spend, and it is possible to imagine how these competing demands might be met differently at different times of the day: the manager of a busy cafe might want to shorten the length of stay of customers during a lunchtime rush, for instance, but encourage customers to linger and

[3] See Andrew Gregory's chapter 'The roles of music in society: the ethnomusicological perspective' in *The Social Psychology of Music.* (Hargreaves and North 1997).

[4] A summary of some of this research is provided by Adrian North and David Hargreaves in the chapter 'Music and consumer behaviour' (1997).

therefore spend more in the afternoon. Thus, music's ability to affect physical movement and to structure time, allowing synchronization of collective behaviour, are important aspects of its use in work, retail, therapeutic, and ritual contexts, as well as for specifically aesthetic ends in dance. Many of these uses of music can be seen as contributing to a more general function, namely the facilitation of social bonding, which is the subject of the next section.

7.1.2 Social bonding

From an evolutionary perspective, music has been likened to physical grooming among primates in that it provides an opportunity for social bonding. The advantage of music over speech, in this respect, is that large groups of people can participate in music-making simultaneously, and all can make a contribution to the collective activity. For example, music's ability to synchronize mood states in large numbers of people promotes coherent behaviour, allowing coordinated collective action. Examples of this are the use of music at ritual events such as the opening and closing ceremonies of the Olympic Games, or at religious occasions.

Further evidence for the role of music in social bonding comes from research into mental disorders, and from studies of the biology of musical activities.[5] Williams Syndrome and Asperger-type autism are two complementary mental disorders that together provide evidence for an association between musicality and sociability: whereas people with Williams Syndrome have mental retardation but high levels of verbal, social, and musical skill, people with Asperger-type autism have an aversion to social interaction, reduced understanding of social emotions (such as guilt, empathy), and may derive little pleasure from music. In a different domain, biological research has identified links between music and hormone release. Oxytocin, associated with social bonding, is released during music listening; conversely, testosterone

---

[5] This argument is presented by David Huron in 'Is music an evolutionary adaptation?' (2003).

levels, associated with aggression and sexual competition, are reduced, which may have the effect of enhancing group cohesion. If music does encourage social bonding, as is suggested by the converging evidence, what psychological processes might underlie this?

Many people believe that music communicates the emotional experiences of a composer and/or performer, or some other intended meaning, to a listener. Such a view is only partially sustainable given the complexity of the processes involved in expressing, perceiving, and experiencing emotion outlined in this chapter and the others before it. However, there are instances where musical and music-related behaviours clearly promote social bonding. The use of infant-directed speech, or 'Motherese', mentioned in Chapter 2, is an interesting example because it illustrates that communication need not rely on verbal information, and can even be more effective than verbal communication in certain situations (such as the therapeutic interactions between music therapists and their clients described later). In the case of infant–caregiver interactions, so crucial to the relationship between child and adult, their turn-taking nature and the sounds that caregivers make (the rhythms and pitches of their vocal utterances) are more important than their semantic content.

Music is also sometimes used in direct communication. For example, some types of music derive from signals used to communicate across distances, where register, volume, and sustained sound carry further than other vocal utterances, and where visual signals are impossible due to the landscape or weather conditions. For example, Norwegian herding music (now performed in concert halls by professional singers) originated in pre-industrial Norwegian farming communities, where women used sound signals in their daily work to keep cattle together and to communicate with other herders working nearby. Music is also used for religious teaching, for example, in parts of Indonesia where the performing arts have been a means of disseminating Islamic thought. Music is a particularly effective means of reaching illiterate populations, and during the civil war in Laos in the 1970s (where there was a very low level of literacy among the local population), both US-backed royalists and Vietnamese-supported Communist factions used traditional vocal music to spread propagandist messages. Censorship and the banning of music on political grounds is further evidence of the belief that music can communicate.

There are a variety of other ways in which musical sound is used to communicate a signal or message. For example, chanting the Koran, or a call to prayer are devices to remind humans of their religious duty. Whereas in epic poetry or folk ballads, music functions as a mnemonic device aiding the preservation and communication of myths, legends, and social mores transgenerationally. Music affords such uses because it helps chunk words and phrases, aiding learning and recall of short fragments of text.[6] Evidence for this comes from studies of jingles in advertising which show that text is easier to remember when sung to a repeated melody.

However, these direct communicative uses of music, in which music functions as a signal or message, are probably rather rare in comparison to aesthetic uses of music. In this context, then, what are the psychological processes that underlie the contribution of music to the construction and communication of the traditions and values of a culture?

7.1.3 Music as the expression of the traditions and values of a culture

The preceding section has focused primarily on the use of music as a signal, or to communicate a verbal message. However, music also embodies values and meanings through the relationships it facilitates, the kinds of physical engagement it elicits, and through the meanings that particular musical materials and practices come to acquire. All of these can be thought of as ways in which music helps to construct and maintain individual and group identity – a topic we return to in Chapter 9.

---

[6] See Wallace (1994). Evidence that jingles are not always effective is provided in Yalch (1991).

Some people identify themselves as 'musicians' – what does this mean? How does it differ from calling oneself a rock guitarist, an mbira player, a composer of electroacoustic music, or a conductor of a church choir? One question that arises from the ways in which individual identity is associated with particular forms of music-making and listening is the extent to which these reflect particular personal attributes.[7] There is some evidence, for instance, that musicians can be characterized, in very general terms, by personality traits. Musicians tend to score highly on measures of introversion, which may be because many forms of musicianship require long periods of working alone and therefore attract those likely to enjoy this. Equally, extended periods of working in isolation may render an individual more introverted over time.

Musical activities may also help to construct and maintain gender, ethnic, cultural, regional, national, and other identities. Studies of the instrument choices of British and American children starting instrumental lessons reveal clear gender distinctions in the instruments children (and adults) believe suitable for boys and girls. So, for example, brass instruments are sometimes assumed to be more suitable for boys perhaps because of their historical associations with the military, and with particular kinds of traditionally male occupations (such as colliery bands in the UK), which in turn arises from their loudness and weather resistance, making them suitable for open air performances. One theory is that these culturally specific gender norms are adopted by children in the process of socialization, such that instrumental preferences even help to shape modes of behaviour. Playing certain instruments or singing involves particular kinds of display, physical movement, interaction, performance venue and occasion, any of which might be considered more or less appropriate for men and women within a culture. For example, singing is regarded as more appropriate activity for women because it is a congruent with associations of the female body with nature (the voice is understood as coming directly from the body, and therefore 'natural' as opposed to the 'technological' symbolism

---

[7] See Kemp's *The Musical Temperament: Psychology and Personality of Musicians* (1996).

of manipulating an instrument). Thus, particular kinds of musical activity can be understood as ways of 'disciplining' the body into gender-appropriate patterns of display, physical movement, and interaction.

But is there anything about the sonic dimension of music that helps maintain or construct identity? Some authors have argued that there is, and that music represents certain kinds of identity by virtue of its specific musical materials, usually in conjunction with explicitly programmatic elements. According to this view, the historical usage of musical material (the historical association of certain musical materials with particular meanings) allows us to hear music as representing people and events in particular ways, with the consequence that Western art music has tended to construct or portray particular views of femininity and masculinity. So, for instance, a transgressive female such as the heroine Carmen, from Bizet's opera of the same name, is given chromatic melodic lines, and gypsy dance forms to sing, which not only signal her dangerously exotic and sexualized otherness within the opera, but also requires her musical annihilation (and therefore her onstage death) in order to achieve tonal and dramatic closure.[8] While music can construct and maintain values and cultural norms of behaviour, this also means that it can be used to critique them, as in Jimi Hendrix's performance of 'The Star Spangled Banner' at the Woodstock music festival in 1969.[9]

Music, then, is one way in which people learn about the values and behaviours appropriate to a culture, but it is also a way in which individuals can construct a sense of who they are. This is perhaps most obvious in everyday conversations about music: people's musical tastes, for instance, are in some sense also a representation, or even a

---

[8] The example of Carmen is discussed by Susan McClary in *Feminine Endings: Music, Gender and Sexuality* (1991). A good overview of gender and music is given by Lucy Green in *Music, Gender, Education* (1997).

[9] The critical character of Jimi Hendrix's performance of 'The Star Spangled Banner' is discussed by Eric Clarke in his book *Ways of Listening: An Ecological Approach to the Perception of Musical Meaning* (2005b).

component, of who they are, which is why arguments over favourite musics can become so heated. There is overwhelming evidence of the importance of musical tastes in constructing identity, particularly for adolescents:[10] their membership of in-groups and out-groups depends more on their music preferences than their prowess in other activities such as sport, and it can be more important to the group that new members are perceived to have the 'right' musical tastes than whether or not they are perceived as boring. According to this view, taste is neither 'natural' nor 'subjective' but is a marker of social distinctions (whether they be distinctions of class, gender, nationality, 'hipness', or any other sort).

Participatory musical activity offers particularly powerful opportunities for sustaining national, cultural, and ethnic identities. All collective music-making requires the coordination and synchronization of a group of people, and therefore enacts in musical processes the very solidarity that group identity implies, whether through the dance practices of the London Sri Lankan Tamil community, parading bands in Northern Ireland, or the singing of a national anthem.

One consequence of music's ability to represent the traditions and values of a culture is that it has the potential to promote understanding of that culture to those who are from other cultures. If music embodies the values and beliefs of a culture through its forms, sonic characteristics, organizational structures, and practices, then learning to play that music, and learning about that music, should promote learning not just about the music, but also about the culture too. In a similar way, songs can be understood not just as artistic creations in their own right but also as a way of gaining insight into someone else's psyche: in other words, a song can be understood as saying 'this is what it's like to be me', where 'me' is the persona projected by the song – which may or may not correspond to that of the composer or performer. To what extent any particular song communicates the reality of what it is like to

---

10 This work on adolescent identity and musical preferences appears alongside a collection of other chapters on music and identity in *Musical Identities* (MacDonald *et al.*, 2002).

be a particular singer or composer is debatable, but regardless of its veracity, the persona offers a means of gaining insight into perhaps identifying with and even 'becoming' for a short period of time, another person. As Stephanie Pitts has shown, this is something that motivates some amateur musicians to take on performing an operatic role, for instance, or in other ways to explore personal characteristics through music that are inaccessible in the rest of their lives.[11]

7.1.4 Using music to target people for commerce and social control

Once musical materials come to be associated with certain values and groups of people, this process can be turned back on itself and used to target certain kinds of people for particular purposes.

> Sarah is shopping for clothes in a high street that she does not know very well: she needs a smart outfit to attend a job interview. As she walks down the street, she hears music coming from some of the shops. She enters a clothes shop and spends a few minutes browsing the tightly packed racks. She is vaguely aware of current top-forty chart hits playing in the background over the shop's sound system. The clothes seem to be aimed at a younger market and are too casual for what she needs. She exits and heads along the street: she walks past a shop with rock music blaring out and a window display of jeans, past a shop playing classical music and a window display of what seem to her frumpy clothes, and on to the next – a shop where the widely spaced clothes rails and designer interior suggest she might find the kind of thing she is looking for. She is the only customer and at first feels slightly uncomfortable under the gaze of the shop assistants, but notices that they are playing a cult-status chillout album from a year or two previously that was a favourite of Sarah's, and quickly gets absorbed in the clothes.

[11] A detailed study of musical participation in a number of different contexts appears in Stephanie Pitts' book *Valuing Musical Participation* (2005a), and in the article "Everyone want to be Pavarotti" (2004).

Walk down any high street or shopping mall, and it is likely that you will hear a variety of musics emanating from the various retail outlets. One effect of this is to attract and repel particular kinds of consumers, where the store and products sold are associated with the 'right' kind of consumer tastes in music. For Sarah, a clothes shop which played loud chart pop music indicated that it sold clothes aimed at the youth market, whereas classical music indicated that the shop sold clothes for older people. If these correspondences seem stereotyped, it is because they are: one consequence of the type of music played in shops is that it targets certain consumers, either because the music really does appeal to the tastes of its desired customers or because the music is a culturally recognized signifier of that target social group, thereby attracting the intended customers and repelling others. The fact that Sarah finally found clothes that she liked in a shop that happened to be playing one of her favourite albums is more than just a coincidence: tastes in fashion and music coalesce as part of who we are, and become tools which can be used to sell to us as customers.

For the same reasons, music can be used to repel certain kinds of people. For example, in an attempt to reduce antisocial behaviour, some subway stations in cities around the world play classical (and sometimes easy listening) music on platforms, and supermarkets in Britain broadcast classical music over loudspeakers outside their premises.[12] This strategy has been effective in reducing vandalism and other unwanted behaviours, apparently because the adolescents responsible in these instances no longer spend time in what they perceive to be a 'less cool' area. The fact that adolescents were discouraged from loitering when the music was playing highlights the way that musical preferences, and the values with which music is associated, can be harnessed.

---

[12] Reports of music used to reduce antisocial behaviour in public spaces include: 'Shops go classical to combat yobs' (BBC News, 2004b), 'Classics deter bus station yobs' (BBC News, 2004c), 'Vandals driven away by loud tunes' (BBC News, 2005a), and 'Classical solution to anti-social behaviour' (BBC News, 2005b), All reported on bbc.co.uk. Consulted 11 May 2005.

Adolescence is generally thought of as the life stage most concerned with identity, and – as we have seen – being associated with the 'wrong' musical preferences can have negative social consequences for in-group membership, and thus self-identity and self-esteem. Music has also been used by interrogators to torture and break down captives prior to interview, by depriving prisoners of sleep through the continual and repeated playing of culturally offensive music.[13]

The idea that lies behind the use of music to attract customers, and to repel troublesome adolescents, is that the shared meanings expressed by particular musics can be put to use to achieve social and commercial ends; thus music serves an important purpose in advertising. As in the example of Sarah, music can influence an individual's purchases by priming the selection of certain products, since the meanings of musical genres are pervasive among members of a particular culture but tend to operate below conscious awareness. So, for instance, when stereotypically French music was played in a supermarket wine display, consumers bought more French wine, and conversely, when stereotypically German music was played, consumers bought more German wine. In this case, consumers (unconsciously) recognized the nationality signified by the music and, via a process in which the music primed other thoughts and associations, then purchased wine produced by that country.[14]

7.1.5 Music in advertising and film

The example of priming cited above is a strong indicator that enculturated listeners hear music as having certain meanings deriving from its history of use in other social contexts and their associated meanings and functions. It is partly these 'sedimented' meanings that enable music to function to powerful effect in multimedia contexts.

---

[13] Use of music in war has been reported in the media (e.g. 'Sesame Street breaks Iraqi POWs' [BBC News, 2003]). A more detailed consideration of music used in war can be found in Suzanne Cusick (2008).

[14] See North *et al.* (1999). However, a similar study by Hume *et al.* (2003) failed to replicate this finding.

Rav is in the cinema waiting for the film to start: the lights are dimmed and he is chatting to a friend rather than paying attention to the adverts and trailers that precede the film. His attention is suddenly drawn by what sounds like a Baroque concerto grosso. The music is tense – a repeated question-and-answer-style phrase over a static bass line, played by a small string ensemble. With his interest aroused by the music, he turns to watch the screen, on which are the silhouettes of two figures. From this contained and mysterious beginning, the music opens up: the isochronous movement is taken up by the whole string ensemble in double time, rising in pitch in regular blocks, and intensified by a crescendo. At the same moment, the figures on the screen come into sharper focus: the silhouette of a man takes the hand of the silhouetted woman, and as the repeated pitch pattern over a dominant pedal spills over into arpeggiated movement on the tonic, the man places a diamond ring on the woman's hand. Rav has been watching an advertisement for diamonds.

One of music's functions in film and television advertising, besides entertaining consumers, is to attract attention, particularly important in contexts where consumers are potentially doing other things at the same time. The onset of music elicits a basic orienting response, and in the context of a ritual event, marks out a temporal and physical space removed from the everyday. In the case of film, television, or video games, music creates a virtual auditory environment, which helps focus attention and draw the listener-viewer in.

Music influences the way that information from advertisements is processed: it captures the attention and provides the cues that help access the listener's product-relevant knowledge. In other words, music is effective in advertising because it communicates meanings about the product. Just as one of the techniques of poster advertising is to juxtapose a product (e.g. perfume) with another desirable object (e.g. a beautiful woman) so music is juxtaposed with a product in such a way that the product takes on the meanings associated in the mind of the listener-viewer with the music. The music used in the De Beers diamond advert described above (first shown in the United Kingdom in 1995), was from Karl Jenkins' *Palladio*, which is a pastiche of a Baroque concerto grosso. The work has many of the same features as its generic model – string orchestration, a small ensemble, regular phrasing and rhythmic structure, balanced antecedent-consequent phrase structure, and limited motivic development – all of which could be regarded as features of Baroque string writing. This functions within the context of the visual imagery to endow the product (in this case diamonds) with particular meanings: class, wealth, and prestige are suggested by virtue of the Baroque pastiche and its referencing of European high art; sexual and romantic union are symbolized by the synchronization of musical tension and release with the visual image of a man placing diamond jewellery on a woman in a prelude to an embrace. The message is one in which the associations of the music are appropriated by the diamond: to buy the diamond is therefore to buy these accrued meanings. In this case the process simultaneously operates in reverse, conferring connotations of wealth and romance on the music, and reaffirming these already sedimented meanings.

In film and advertising, music also provides the more straightforward function of continuity, taking advantage of the perceptual integration of auditory and visual information to cover over the disruption of rapid cuts between different camera shots and discontinuities in the visual and verbal narrative. Listen carefully to television adverts and you will come across non-sequiturs in the voice-over such as 'Is love eternal? New everlasting X Factor Mascara gives you longer lashes': juxtapositions such as these seem ludicrous in print, but in the context of music and visuals the absence of logic in such 'arguments' is much less noticeable.

But are people really as susceptible to the influences of musical advertising as this would seem to suggest? The classical conditioning effect, in which preference for a product increases with liking for the music with which it is paired, only seems to be effective when people have no reason to evaluate the advertised brand; when people have the ability, motivation, and opportunity to process information about the advertised product then they are less likely to be influenced by their liking for the music.[15]

7.2 **Therapeutic applications of music**

Music is commonly used in therapeutic situations, both by professional practitioners, and by individuals as a self-administered therapeutic tool. Therapeutic uses of music, then, encompass any uses of music that meet the restorative needs of a person, whether in the context of formal therapy involving a qualified practitioner, or various kinds of musical behaviour undertaken by individuals to meet their own needs without the intervention of a therapist. Using music to relax, to help exercise, and to manage social situations are just a few of the ways in which people use music as self-therapy. It is not the aim of this section to provide a survey of therapeutic uses of music[16] but to suggest in more general terms how music might function therapeutically. We ask what the therapeutic effects of music are, if they are underpinned by the same psychological principles, and why and how they occur.

7.2.1 **Informal therapeutic uses of music**

Just as listening to music can have therapeutic benefits so too performing music can be beneficial to people's well-being. Lying somewhere midway along the continuum of informal to formal therapeutic applications of music (or 'self-therapy' to 'medical and therapeutic applications') are the therapeutic possibilities of amateur music-making.

---

[15] See Park and Young (1986).

[16] For accounts of music therapy, see Bunt (1994), Ansdell (1995), Pavlicevic (1997), and Pavlicevic and Ansdell (2004).

David lives in Montreal, Canada, and until recently had been home-less for two years. Six months ago, he heard about a choir for home-less men and became a member. Like many in the choir, David has emotional disorders, has suffered from alcohol and drug abuse, has been unemployed for many years, and finds it difficult to sustain relationships. The choir began by singing Christmas carols to passers-by in a subway station, but since then have performed at numerous concerts, appeared on television, and made CDs. They now sing an eclectic repertoire, including French-Canadian folk songs, pop songs, hymns, and classical music. Since joining the choir, David's life and those of others like him have changed dramatically: all now live in permanent housing, some have found part-time work, and most now have much more stable living circumstances.

The remarkable true story of 'David's' involvement in a choir for homeless men is illustrative of the wide range of therapeutic benefits that can arise out of musical participation.[17] Participation in a group activity allowed David and the other men opportunities for structured but flexible social interactions with each other, with the leader(s) of the choir, and subsequently with their audiences. Musical rehearsal and performance necessarily engaged these men in communicating musical intentions and developed their communication skills and ability to cooperate over the course of the rehearsals. Other benefits of group participation reported by the men included a sense of belonging, not only to the choir itself but also to the wider community, and opportunities for intense and fulfilling aesthetic and emotional experiences.

---

[17] This research is reported by Betty Bailey and Jane Davidson (2002). See Pitts (2005a) for a detailed account of the experience of amateur music-making in a number of different settings. Pitts identifies several motivations for musical participation which are mentioned by Bailey and Davidson as being benefits of participation in the choir for homeless men: as a source of confirmation and confidence, as an opportunity to acquire and demonstrate skills, to preserve and promote a repertoire, as an opportunity to perform with others, as a forum for social interaction and friendships, as an escape from or enhancement of the everyday, for spiritual fulfilment and pleasure.

Their self-esteem increased as a result of feeling that they were contributing to something that was valued by the public who came to their concerts, appreciated their performances and who bought their recordings, and encouraged them to feel pride in their activities. The mental engagement entailed by singing in the choir exercised the men's concentration, provided cognitive stimulation, and structured their thought processes during rehearsals and performances. In addition, some of the men reported that participation had increased their emotional awareness and sensitivity and given them an opportunity to explore and heal emotional wounds. The therapeutic benefits of amateur choral singing are particularly visible in the case of the dramatic changes that took place in the quality of life of this group of homeless men, but many of these same effects are reported by other kinds of amateur music-makers.

People who participate in music-making often say that it provides them with opportunities for self-expression, but what does this really mean? Singing, making instrumental music, performing as a soloist or in a group, or making a compilation of recordings can all be classed as self-expression, because they have in common an act of creativity with musical materials, whether pre-recorded, improvised, or played/sung from notation. They all enable people to harness the meanings that the music has for them and to experience them directly through their manipulation of musical sound and practice. In some instances, music acts as a release for otherwise inexpressible emotions or ideas, perhaps as an expression of protest or as the enactment of a form of personal comfort. For example, the narratives of female mistreatment in twentieth century Bulgarian song, sung by women, express a fear of mistreatment by men, whether or not they are actually mistreated. These songs were not sung in public as a form of protest, but were sung as consolation during times of stress.[18]

----

[18] This example of female song in Bulgaria is taken from Timothy Rice's book *May it Fill Your Soul: Experiencing Bulgarian Music* (1994).

A second common form of self-therapy is focussed on listening to music, particularly in contemporary industrialized societies where personal mobile listening devices are now widely available. Besides the numerous social and emotional functions of music listening already discussed, it is increasingly used – and not only by individuals wearing headphones – to create private space within an increasingly populated public realm. So, for instance, music can be broadcast in public spaces in order to mask the sounds of other people. Recall Sarah's experience of walking into a store where she was the only customer. The presence of music reduced her self-consciousness as she browsed the racks, and heightened her sense of privacy. Similarly, for people working in open plan spaces, or sitting on trains or buses, music creates a controlled auditory environment in the form of accompanied isolation when listened to via mobile, individualized listening technologies. Although such 'privatized' public space may improve an individual's mood and well-being, one consequence is a public realm in which social interaction is minimized. New, networked digital technologies are changing the way in which people communicate and experience sound and space. The ability to hear sound from a different time and space, first made possible with the introduction of sound recording and reproduction technology over a hundred years ago, means that virtual worlds and spaces are superimposed onto the real environment. Just how these virtual environments will change listening and music-making is only just beginning to be explored, but they raise questions about how people understand virtual spaces and virtual communication and their impact on musical and other kinds of experience.

7.2.2 Medical and formal therapeutic uses of music

Music has long been used for a wide variety of medical and therapeutic purposes directed at improving physical, mental, social, and emotional well-being. Music is able to facilitate this by drawing on a whole range of mechanisms, outlined in this subsection, and this is reflected in the different types of music therapy on offer and the many ways in which music therapy can benefit people with very different needs.

One important difference between the uses of music in self-therapy and the practices of professional music therapists is that therapy is not just a manipulation of psychological or physical states, but a way of helping individuals to develop more appropriate (more functional) responses to problems. Music therapy, as opposed to the informal therapeutic use of music, describes the activities of practitioners who work with clients who need assistance in dealing with specific physical and/or psychological difficulties. Music therapy, as it is practiced in the industrialized nations of the Western world, involves two main types of interaction using music: a receptive approach, in which the client listens to live or recorded music played by the therapist, and a participatory approach, in which patients improvise, often one-to-one, or in a small group with a therapist.[19] In Guided Imagery and Music, a therapeutic approach developed by Helen Bonney, for instance, music acts as a catalyst to evoke unconscious thoughts and feelings in a client and to expand their self-awareness. The therapist selects music to attain deep relaxation and to guide the client towards certain imagery before engaging in drawing and talking with the aim of integrating insights gained into the client's daily life. By contrast, the active improvised music therapy approach, such as that developed by Paul Nordoff and Clive Robbins, uses a technique in which the client is encouraged to improvise with the therapist, who listens to, stimulates, and responds to the client and tries to 'meet' him or her in a musical-therapeutic relationship. For example, a therapeutic session with a client who is aggressive with others may focus on extending that person's musical expressive range. If the client plays at a fast tempo, the therapist plays slower, and so on. By extending his or her musical expressive range, it is hoped that the client will experience themself differently and be able to draw on this new expressive range in everyday life.

Focusing on the potential of music to influence emotional well-being, how might music work as a therapeutic device in the case of treating a pathological affective state, for instance? There is potential for music to

---

[19] See Gary Ansdell's *Music for Life: Aspects of Creative Music Therapy with Adult Clients.* (1995).

work via a number of different mechanisms: social and cognitive mechanisms, such as appraisal, empathy, mastery, affirmation of identity, group experience, sense of belonging, focus on the present, and cognitive priming; physiological mechanisms, through the 'coupling' of physiological systems with the musical environment; and even biochemical mechanisms. Take the example of depression, for instance. Depression is a cycle of negative cognitions, and anomalous states of arousal. Thus, extrinsic musical cues, either produced in improvisation, or present in pre-composed music played by the therapist, can trigger the recall of situations, scenarios, people, and emotions outside the pathological state, while intrinsic musical processes can raise or lower arousal appropriate to the individual and context.

Some of the same processes underlying the use of music for relaxation and anxiety reduction also underlie the use of music in clinical settings to reduce pain. Music has been found to be particularly effective for dental patients and those with chronic pain, but why should this be? Pain is multifaceted, comprising physiological, psychological, and social aspects, so there are many ways in which music may reduce the experience of pain. One possibility is that music stimulates an endorphin response, which acts as an endogenous opiate – a spontaneously secreted analgesic. However, music interventions are not always associated with an increase in endorphins. Physiological measures and verbal self-reports suggest that music interventions also reduce anxiety and increase muscle relaxation, and this may reduce expectations of pain and catastrophizing thoughts, and distract an individual from the experience of pain. A second clue to music's effectiveness lies in evidence that music is much more effective in pain relief when it has been chosen by the individuals themselves. This supports the findings of other studies showing that the experience of pain is reduced in circumstances where the person experiences more control.

Participatory music therapy, described above, can also benefit an individual's physical and social functioning. As discussed in Chapter 2, musical performance requires a range of motor skills, and the use of music in settings where people have physical impairments therefore brings with it the opportunity to address and attempt to develop people's specific physical capacities. Just as physiotherapy may aim to improve aspects of physical control, such as the control of force, and of spatial and temporal accuracy, so music-making requires the exercise of these same skills, but in a potentially intrinsically enjoyable and motivating setting. Where other forms of communication are difficult, the shared coordination in sound and movement that occurs in music-making may be an important medium for social interaction, since a crucial feature of musical communication is that it involves the establishment and management of relationships. It is for these reasons that improvisation has been such a central component of professional music therapy in the United Kingdom. And yet many questions remain. What exactly is the relationship between music and therapy within music therapy? And if the therapy is 'mostly musical', how is it possible to explain this to a client, doctor, or funding agency? Although the positive benefits of professional music therapy are not in doubt, there is still much to be understood about the nature and basis of its effectiveness and the psychological and musical processes that it involves.

7.3 Music and evolution

Perhaps the most fundamental question to ask about the uses of music is why, and under what circumstances human beings first began to make music. From the perspective of evolution by natural selection, musical behaviours may have conferred an advantage on our human ancestors. On the basis that natural selection determines the genetically based behaviours that are passed on to subsequent generations, there are two main arguments regarding the adaptive value of music.[20] On the one hand, current theories of evolutionary psychology hold that natural selection has resulted in a human mind consisting of mental modules the purpose of which is to address specific adaptive needs such as the ability to recognize and respond to physical objects and forces, and understand other human minds. This has led some writers to claim

---

[20] These arguments are presented by David Huron (2003). See also Ian Cross's chapter 'Music and biocultural evolution' (2003).

that music is parasitic on human capacities which have developed for other evolutionarily adaptive purposes, but which human beings exploit for the non-adaptive pleasure they provide – a view epitomized by Steven Pinker's claim that 'music is auditory cheesecake, an exquisite confection crafted to tickle the sensitive spots of at least six of our mental faculties'.[21] In other words, music may not directly influence survival, but may exploit ways to experience pleasure that have an adaptive origin.

On the other hand, music may have been selectively advantageous at an earlier stage of human development, and may retain aspects of those functions. Steven Mithen has argued that spoken language may have originated from a musical proto-language expressive of emotion.[22] He argues that the development of a more sophisticated social organization, more complex tools and higher arts, which took place approximately 40,000 years ago – and which coincides with evidence for the first musical instruments – were the result of cognitive developments in individuals such that the modules of the mind, previously independent, became accessible to one another. It may even be the case that the flourishing of musical and other artistic activities at this time actually facilitated these cognitive developments.

The extent to which music has adaptive value is still being investigated, but two possibilities have been suggested: first, that music facilitates development of the individual human mind by integrating information of different types and, second, that it affords interaction between human beings by reinforcing group identity and group morale, for example, releasing individual tensions without destroying group cohesion and allowing coordinated social activity in a manner that is unlikely to involve conflict.[23] So some of the theories about how music

---

[21] See Steven Pinker's book *How the Mind Works* (1997), p.534.

[22] See Steven Mithen's book *The Singing Neanderthals: The Origins of Music, Language, Mind and Body* (2005).

[23] The adaptive value of music is discussed in Steven Mithen's books *The prehistory of the Mind: the Cognitive Origins of Art, Religion, and Science* (1996), and *The Singing Neanderthals: The Origins of Music, Language, Mind and Body* (2005); and in Ian Cross's chapter '*Is music the most important thing we ever did? Music, development and evolution*' (1999).

confers an adaptive advantage overlap with the contemporary uses of music discussed above, although others have a less obvious connection. For example, music may have arisen as courtship behaviour (perhaps being able to sing well was an indication of an individual's good health), and listening to or performing music may have brought about improvements in auditory skills, or motor coordination. Music may have fostered group cohesion, or enabled group synchronization, improving the effectiveness of collective action, and it may have acted as an effective way of passing on useful information, for example, through songs. Music may also have reduced conflict by providing a collective social activity, or simply provided a safe way to pass time, keeping our human ancestors out of harm's way when otherwise unoccupied.

7.4 Reflections on using music

The multiple uses of music, and their overlapping consequences, reveal the rich affordances of music for human beings. These arise from the interplay of three features: the auditory character of music, which means that it can be listened to and made while engaged in concurrent activities; its varied forms of participation through playing, composing and listening; and the potential it offers for individual and collective experience. This and the previous two chapters have explored this array of uses by focusing on the psychological processes behind a range of the more general musical functions: entertainment, aesthetic enjoyment and self-actualization; emotional experience; communication; the representation and construction of the values, patterns, and themes of a culture; the enhancement of human development and task performance; and therapeutic applications. We have not attempted to discuss all possible uses of music, nor to account exhaustively for all the functions music serves in those examples that we have presented; but what we hope to have done is to have illustrated the ways in which psychological theories of attention, arousal, affect, time perception, motor skill, social interaction, and

---

A third alternative to the adaptation versus byproduct debate has been proposed by Aniruddh Patel, who argues that music is a biologically powerful invention - a 'transformative technology' of the mind.

identity can help to explain the multitude of ways in which music is used, and some of the consequences of those uses.

As was pointed out in the introduction to Chapter 5, the utilitarian perspective that is implied by the term 'using music' goes against prevailing views of art music in the West. Disproportionate attention has been given by researchers in music perception and cognition to understanding focused listening by comparison with background listening. It is unclear to what extent conclusions about listening in other contexts can be drawn from existing research in music perception and cognition, almost all of which has been carried out in laboratory-style focused listening circumstances, and so questions remain about how people hear and understand music in contexts where music is not the primary focus.

Arguably, it is no coincidence that the same industrialized nations where this research takes place also market music under the rubric of functionality. Compilations of 'mood music' or 'music to improve your IQ' incorporate music from diverse genres with apparently little regard for musical specificities. Some writers have claimed that the tendency to treat all music as if it has the same uses is a serious problem in contemporary culture and indicates that people have lost the ability to understand music on its own terms and for the things that it can offer, which do not fall neatly into these functional categories.[24] These are serious and provocative arguments that demand attention rather than either simple dismissal or hasty agreement. Both the ideology of musical autonomy, and a perspective on music's functions that focuses only on its collateral effects, unwittingly deny music its full significance in contemporary life.

---

[24] For a discussion, see Julian Johnson's book *Who Needs Classical Music* (2002).

Part 3

Acquiring music

Much of the focus in this book so far has been on adults: we have considered the ways in which people make music through performance, composition, and improvisation; how they use and respond to music; the psychological processes involved in understanding and perceiving music; and the extent to which music contributes to fulfilling emotional and social needs. We now turn to considering how the foundations for such behaviour are laid: how interest in music is fostered through home, school, and broader social environments, and how musical skills and understanding are acquired, more or less deliberately, in those contexts.

The topic of how people acquire musical understanding is addressed here from two perspectives. First, Chapter 8 considers the development of musical skills throughout people's lives, while taking account of maturational processes, including the potential decline of physical skills in late adulthood. Chapter 9 then examines the contexts for musical learning, looks at the influences and processes in deliberate musical education – whether directed by a teacher or by the learners themselves – and draws comparisons with the more casual acquisition of music through daily exposure, which has been discussed elsewhere in this book. Both chapters draw on research within music education and music psychology, and evaluate the extent to which each discipline can inform the other in attempting to understand how musical skills, knowledge, and attitudes are acquired, and how they can best be nurtured and encouraged.

Chapter 8

Lifelong musical development

8.1 Maturational processes in acquiring music

From the earliest days of virtually all children's lives, listening and responding to sound are central to their interactions with adults, contributing to socialization and well-being, and beginning the process of acquiring musical skills and understanding. Communicating with babies through encounters that can loosely be called musical seems to be instinctive: it forms the basis of the 'motherese' that caregivers use to talk to infants (see Chapter 2) and underpins the use of lullabies to soothe babies, musical toys to stimulate them, and later, action songs and nursery rhymes to involve children in music-making. Musical and linguistic interactions alike help infants to form social relationships and to acquire a sense of self, such that music is seen by some researchers as being essential to effective social functioning by providing a low-risk forum for trying out communication and other kinds of social competences.[1] Music is as much a part of everyday life for young children as it is for adults, and many of its functions are similar: regulating mood, creating a sense of involvement, providing fun and enjoyment, and affirming identity and belonging. The main difference is that young children are still acquiring perceptual and motor skills, and according to their age and musical experience will bring to their listening and responding different levels of melodic, rhythmic, and harmonic awareness, of singing, clapping, and playing, of emotional understanding, and of cultural reference.

---

[1] Colwyn Trevarthen's work on mother–infant communication is among the most well known, and he gives a summary of his work in the chapter 'Origins of musical identity: evidence from infancy for musical social awareness' in *Musical Identities* (edited by Raymond MacDonald, David Hargreaves & Dorothy Miell, 2002).

Babies' receptiveness to music is in place even before they are born: hearing develops early in prenatal maturation, with the foetal auditory system able to process sounds from around 20 weeks of gestation, and responses to sound as observed via the foetal heart rate and movement becoming more consistent in the latter half of pregnancy. There has been much recent interest in whether this early auditory development can be used to stimulate prenatal learning: there is some evidence that music heard in the womb is remembered and recognized by newborn babies, but the effects on longer-term learning are minimal, and are far outweighed by more deliberate musical effort and practice in later childhood.[2]

In all areas of musical competence, development is gradual and can be accelerated by opportunities to explore and practise musical concepts through play and training. It is also culturally specific, being affected by the tonal and formal conventions of the music with which the child is surrounded. Research on child development has often chosen to set aside these influences in order to establish a general framework that shows the typical sequence for acquisition of skills and perception. Much of the research in this area has been experimental, using methods and musical materials designed to isolate and measure perceptual skills. One such approach is the 'head-turning' method used with young babies, which takes advantage of the strong inclination of young infants to turn to look at objects and events that interest them. In a typical study, sounds are presented through one of two loudspeakers placed at either side of the baby and his or her caregiver, and researchers monitor the baby's reaction by noting when and for how long a new sound captures his or her attention. These head movements and the baby's direction of gaze can indicate musical preferences for changes in timbre, rhythm, phrasing, tonality, and so on, and repeated testing with large numbers of participants can begin to establish the norms of perception and response.

---

[2] Richard Parncutt provides a summary of the literature on prenatal development in his chapter in Gary McPherson's *The Child as Musician: A Handbook of Musical Development* (2006).

Through research using these head-turning methods, infants have been shown to have an acute sense of pitch discrimination, being able to detect differences of a semitone or less, and to show preferences for consonant over dissonant intervals. Young infants are more flexible in their perception of metre than are adults, who have been enculturated into particular metrical preferences, according to their musical surroundings and experience. The effects of such enculturation have also been studied experimentally in rather reduced but more controlled circumstances: babies who listened to a metrically ambiguous drum pattern were bounced on either the second or third beat of the pattern, and subsequently showed a preference for performances that emphasized the same beat as had been marked out through the bouncing pattern.[3] This experiment, mirroring the commonplace parenting behaviour of moving babies to music before they are capable of making an independent physical response, shows how emerging musical perception is affected by social and cultural contexts. Children are predisposed to acquiring music, and do so according to an underlying maturational sequence, but this is strongly influenced by their individual experiences and the musical behaviour of those around them.

Once children are able to respond verbally or physically to musical stimuli, research can be undertaken using a greater variety of experimental measures. Studies of rhythm perception, for instance, might require children to tap along with a given pattern, or to repeat it through clapping or playing. The ability to move to given rhythms, and subsequently to match and imitate them, grows during the preschool years, although it is often sustained only for brief periods of time, again increasing with age. Research in rhythm development has to take account of other maturational factors, because children's abilities to respond to a rhythmic task may be affected by simple physical strength and coordination, such that their overt behaviour may not be a fair reflection of their aural ability. David Hargreaves notes that some

---

3 For further details of research with infants, see Sandra Trehub's chapter on 'Infants as musical connoisseurs' in Gary McPherson's *The Child as Musician: A Handbook of Musical Development* (2006).

studies found that children's capacities appeared to improve over an experimental session lasting half an hour or so, which casts some doubt on the reliability of brief tests administered only once or twice.[4]

Although attempts to generalize about the acquisition of musical skills and perception are complicated by the highly individual circumstances in which young children come to know and experience music, a variety of studies have nonetheless been able to determine some broad sequences of musical acquisition, within which individual differences can be recognized and accommodated. Rhythmic skills are generally agreed to be the first to be established, with very young children able to detect rhythmic changes and to tap or move in time with a rhythm, at least for a short period of time. Pitch discrimination is also evident in children as young as six months, who in one study were able to detect out-of-tune notes in both Western and Javanese scales, showing quite flexible pitch perception capacities that later become more fixed by the specific cultural context within which the child is exposed to music.[5] This would explain why such pitch discrimination tasks are harder for adults: their listening skills have narrowed so that they can make finer discriminations in the context of familiar music but are less able to do so when presented with music in an unfamiliar genre. Young children's melodic understanding has been tested through listening and singing tasks, revealing that memory for the contour of a melody is established before the finer discrimination of pitch intervals. Children gain and can reproduce a rough impression of a nursery song, for instance, without getting too bogged down in the accuracy of precise pitches – sometimes completing phrases with improvised solutions where recall fails them. This, too, is an area of musical competence in which adults become less willing to take risks, both as a result of increasing social anxiety around

---

[4] David Hargreaves' *The Developmental Psychology of Music* (1986) offers an overview of developmental research to that date; a more recent summary is provided by Heiner Gembris in a chapter on 'The development of musical abilities' in the *MENC Handbook of Musical Cognition and Development* (2006). See also Irène Deliège & John Sloboda (Eds.) *Musical Beginnings: Origins and Development of Musical Competence* (1996).

[5] See Lynch and Eilers (1991). Extensive research on the effects of cultural exposure to infants' listening has also been carried out by Laurel Trainor and Sandra Trehub (e.g. Trainor & Trehub, 1992).

singing and because a greater implicit knowledge of harmony makes musical errors more perceptible and inhibiting. Harmonic understanding is the last musical element to stabilize in children's development, generally agreed to emerge at around the age of seven, and to be further refined over a period of years.[6]

> At 8.30 on a Tuesday morning, four-year-old William is watching children's breakfast television, the volume turned up high in the usual hubbub of the family getting ready to go out to work and nursery. As his mum tries to hustle him back up to his bedroom to finish getting dressed, he sings snatches of the theme tune, gradually departing from the 'real' melody and changing the words to suit his current actions – 'Putting my socks on, my socks on, my socks on ...' In the car twenty minutes later, after dropping William at nursery, Alison realizes that she has 'caught' her son's song, although she hums it more quietly under her breath and stops when she notices what she is doing, turning on the car radio instead.

Comparisons of children's emergent musical skills with those of the general adult population show how dependent musical development is upon opportunity and teaching, if latent levels of competence are to retain their potential and flourish into adult life. The vast majority of children have the ability to sing, to recall and reproduce melodies, and to assimilate the music they hear into spontaneous tunes of their own – yet most adults would be much more reticent about doing the same in the presence of other people (although they might be happy enough to sing along to music in the privacy of their car or shower).

6 Heiner Gembris (2006) notes a trend for more recent studies to show harmonic preference and stability emerging in younger children, citing Zenatti's (1993) work in which 6 year olds showed consistent preference for consonant harmonisation of unfamiliar melodies. Gembris suggests that increased mass media exposure is causing earlier enculturation to the Western major-minor tonal system; it could also be the case that the greater volume of research evidence now available is causing researchers to re-think earlier developmental theories.

Reluctance to sing is often evident by the time children start secondary school, when self-consciousness and the desire to please peers rather than teachers is compounded by vocal changes, along with a growing awareness of how the high production values of contemporary pop are markedly different from the embarrassing experience of singing among classmates. Some children, encouraged by parents and teachers, do of course pursue their musical development into these teenage years and beyond – and so the gap widens between those who 'are' musical and those who 'aren't'. The myth that musical skill is a 'gift' or 'talent' that only a few people have is therefore perpetuated, even though the developmental evidence shows that the starting point for musical competence is roughly similar for everyone and that the differences emerge through opportunity, guidance, and inclination.

Research in musical development has been dominated by a focus on listening and perception, but there are some notable exceptions, including Coral Davies' studies of children's invented songs and the notation devised to record them. Working with five to seven year olds in two infant schools, Davies encouraged the children to make up songs, and observed the ways in which they often drew on simple musical forms (AABA or ABAC) to introduce tension and resolution, and at other times developed more extended 'story songs' in which ideas were developed and connected to produce a more or less satisfying musical whole. The children's musical inventions demonstrated an emergent understanding of form, tonality, and rhythm, as well as of the potential for self-expression and communication in music. Some of the children had only a limited inclination to repeat and refine their spontaneous songs, improvising in the moment and beginning a new (although sometimes similar) song rather than reworking a previous attempt. Analysis of the songs shows the children typically working within two or four bar phrases, using repetition and transformation of material within a song, and borrowing from the structures, although not necessarily the melodic contours, of songs known to them. Davies suggests that the musical knowledge demonstrated in the children's songs is far beyond that which they would be able to articulate, and shows an intuitive understanding of musical structure and significance to have been established by the age of seven.[7]

Other studies of children's composing include the 'spiral of musical development', proposed by Keith Swanwick and June Tillman,[8] which shows children progressing from a 'sensory' exploration of musical materials (typically at 0–3 years of age), through 'manipulative' and then 'personally expressive' phases (4–6 years), before showing increasing knowledge of musical conventions and expressive intention in later childhood, and finally reaching the 'symbolic' and 'systematic' stages of musical maturity (15 years and beyond). Swanwick and Tillman's model has been criticized (like Piaget's more general theories of development, to which it relates closely) for its use of age-related stages, although in subsequent defences of the model Swanwick has asserted its flexibility, stating that new musical experiences and challenges will cause older learners to drop down the spiral from their general level of attainment and go through the same sequence of exploration and mastery as they extend their musical skills and horizons. With these modifications, the model is useful as a description of what typically occurs in the compositional development of a child exposed to the current style of music teaching in Britain, although it has more limited value in its claims to generalize beyond composing to wider musical development.

Observing children's musical behaviour in 'real-world' settings, such as their home environments or music classes, can provide different perspectives on the extent to which children have assimilated musical conventions from their everyday exposure, although the information may be harder to interpret in comparison to that gathered through the

---

[7] Coral Davies' studies are presented in two articles in the *British Journal of Music Education*: 'Listen to my song' (1992), and 'Say it till a song comes' (1986).

[8] For a full explanation of the spiral, see Swanwick and Tillman (1986), 'The sequence of musical development: a study of children's composition'. For Swanwick's response to subsequent criticisms of the spiral, see his conference keynote speech from the 2001 Research in Music Education conference, 'Musical developmental theories revisited', published in *Music Education Research*.

systematic tests of pitch and rhythm described earlier in the chapter. It is difficult to achieve a balance between isolating musical elements for systematic study and observing the complexities of everyday musical behaviour, and this presents a challenge for research in child development that can only really be resolved by 'triangulation': comparing the results of multiple studies conducted using a variety of methods. Researchers in this area acknowledge the contradictions between the findings of different studies, and there is much still to be discovered about the variety of ways in which children acquire and perceive music at an early age, and about the effects of early exposure on longer-term musical development, attitudes, and identity.

8.2 **Acquiring a musical identity**

The previous section has shown that the acquisition of musical perception and skill occurs as part of general development: almost all humans develop musical awareness and musical skills, and as such can be expected to express a preference for particular repertoire, to sing along (whatever the quality of the sound) to familiar tunes, or to interpret the emotional function of a film soundtrack. The few exceptions to this are those with a physical or neurological impairment, such as deafness, that inhibits musical development – although Evelyn Glennie's successful career as a solo percussionist, despite her deafness, shows that this is not always a barrier to musical enjoyment and expertise. Individuals with 'amusia' are less likely to overcome their condition and succeed musically, because they have a cognitive deficit that makes them unable to recognize or reproduce some musical features. Amusia is something of an umbrella term, referring to a range of musical deficits, but amusics are typically unable to recognize familiar melodies if they are presented without words and cannot detect differences between melodies, lacking the capacity that is otherwise widespread in the population to hear 'wrong' notes. The absence of pitch-discrimination skills in amusics, despite normal speech processing, suggests the presence of certain neural networks that are specific to music processing (as discussed in Chapter 5) – a theory reinforced by the experience of brain-damaged patients, whose speech processing might be impaired while music processing remains intact, or vice versa. Some estimates suggest that up to 5% of the population is affected by amusia, although the condition often goes unrecognized because the absence of musical sensitivity is covered up by the individual, or attributed to lack of teaching or effort.[9]

For the 95% of the population born with fully functioning auditory and musical capacities, the extent of their development is determined as much by opportunity, motivation, and interest as by the notions of 'talent' that often pervade discussions of performing skill, in particular. However, when only a small proportion of the population engages in the hours of systematic practice that are necessary to acquire high-level mastery of a musical instrument, it is perhaps inevitable that their resultant skills will seem mysterious and unattainable to other people who have not pursued this type of training to anything like the same extent. The question 'is everyone musical?' is one which cultural policy and practice often implicitly answers in the negative, by making musical education optional (as in the UK curriculum after the age of 14), specialist (as in many other European countries), or the preserve of those who can afford individual lessons (as in the case of instrumental tuition in the United Kingdom and elsewhere), and by affording top-level performers the status of celebrities, as demonstrated by high ticket prices, celebrity talent shows, and more general media attention. Researchers in music psychology have answered the same question much more affirmatively, stating that everyone *is* musical in a broad developmental sense, and that variations in opportunities, motivations, and encouragement to foster this musicality are the main determinants of individual musical difference.

John Sloboda and colleagues have questioned the 'folk psychology of talent', which assumes that an innate level of musical skill renders some individuals more musically talented than others. They assert that conclusive evidence for the effects of inherited differences does not

---

[9] See Isabelle Peretz's work with congenital amusics at http://www.brams.umontreal.ca/plab/downloads/PeretzHyde03.pdf and case studies of amusic individuals in *Musicophilia*, by Oliver Sacks (2007).

exist, and propose the alternative view: musical development is a species-defining characteristic, priming all humans to become musicians, just as we are all predisposed to learn language and movement.[10] Some individuals undeniably acquire greater levels of technical and expressive skill in music during their lifetime, but the potential exists for all children to build upon the emergent musical capacities that are evident across the population in the first months of life. Nonetheless, the notion persists that some people are innately 'musical' while others are not, and this in turn becomes a self-fulfilling prophecy, whereby those children encouraged to think of themselves as musical will continue in their efforts to develop those skills and those labelled 'unmusical' will come to believe that they do not have the capacity for musical learning, and abandon any attempt to learn.

The acquisition of musical skill, then, requires encouragement and opportunity early in life in order to give children the time and inclination to amass the hours of instrumental practice necessary for musical accomplishment. This is most obviously true for classical performance, where the demanding motor skills of piano or violin playing, for instance, benefit from an early start (although pedagogical wisdom varies as to exactly when that should be). Other kinds of performance, such as the guitar playing and songwriting associated with the teenage years, might start somewhat later, and while there are no immovable barriers to learning in adult life, acquiring the unfamiliar motor skills needed for many instruments may be more of a challenge to learners who come to them later in life, with their bodily development and motor habits already set into well-established patterns. Whatever the circumstances, acquiring musical skill demands effort and persistence, whether the motivation to do so comes from encouraging parents, demanding teachers, or a self-directed determination to succeed. In other words, the acquisition of musical skill has to be valued and recognized by the child and those around him or her in order to sustain the effort needed to make progress.

----

[10] For an article designed to stimulate debate on this question, see John Sloboda, Jane Davidson & Michael Howe, 'Is everyone musical?', *The Psychologist* (1994). See also Chapters 16 and 17 of John Sloboda's book *Exploring the Musical Mind* (2005).

Learning a musical instrument is one route to acquiring a sense of musical identity: practising and making music become activities for which a child or teenager is known, within the family, school, and beyond, perhaps reinforced through public performances, the achievement of passing exams, and decisions about whether music might form a significant part of an individual's future education and even career. The high level of support offered by parents when performing is seen as a 'hobby' can be confusingly withdrawn when a young person decides to aim for the uncertain world of a musical career.[11] Musical identities are fragile things – as witnessed by the large number of children who begin instrumental tuition but cease on starting secondary school or entering examination years, when the pressures of academic homework mean that music assumes a lower priority in their lives. For adolescent musicians making decisions about their musical futures, the attitudes of parents and teachers can be crucial in shaping the belief system by which teenagers evaluate their musical potential. Although some will have the confidence to view all performing experiences – even an unsuccessful competition, for instance – as formative in their learning, others will be overwhelmed by the pressure to succeed, and will be negatively influenced by criticism from teachers or significant others. A strong self-belief and a range of coping strategies have been shown to be essential to acquiring a secure musical identity in school, higher education, and the professional world, with long-term effects on young musicians' futures as performers.[12]

Acquiring the skills of a classical performer is a somewhat rarefied route to developing a musical identity, and many more individuals identify strongly with music than are represented by the small percentage of the population who attain high levels of performing expertise.

---

[11] An example of this can be found in Sophia Borthwick and Jane Davidson's chapter 'Developing a child's identity as a musician: a family "script" perspective' (pp. 60–78) in *Musical Identities* edited by Raymond MacDonald, David Hargreaves & Dorothy Miell (2002).

[12] For a summary of the musical identity literature and further discussion of the 'coping strategies' needed for performing success, see Jane Davidson & Karen Burland's 'Musician identity formation' (pp. 475–490) in *The Child as Musician: A Handbook of Musical Development* edited by Gary McPherson (2006).

Musical identity has been studied extensively in relation to teenagers' musical behaviour, where peers and siblings are strongly influential in shaping tastes and activities, and choice of music has implications for the broader expression of social values and affiliations. While young children are 'open-eared' and responsive to a wide range of musical styles and genres, adolescents typically express stronger preferences for a narrower repertoire, often moving away from the commercial pop music of their early teens in search of more distinctive individual tastes. Positive and negative attitudes to music tend to be expressed most strongly in front of peers, showing that for this age group (as discussed in Chapter 7), musical behaviour is an important part of self-identity and the search for group approval and membership. Studies have repeatedly shown that musical taste is taken as an indicator of broader character and behaviour: stereotypically negatively valued music for teenagers, such as classical or country and western, brings with it an assumption that listeners will be boring and compliant in school, whereas pop and dance music connote being fun, fashionable, and popular.[13] As such biases are less evident in adult life, it seems clear that individual musical preferences gradually supersede these in-group affiliations, but so far there has been little investigation of that transition and its links with the changing friendship patterns of post-compulsory education and the move into work.

8.3 Learning from exceptional musical development

Another approach to understanding how the capacity for music develops is to analyse the behaviour of those with exceptional musical skills, and to consider what these unusual cases can demonstrate about how

---

[13] Summaries of the literature on adolescent musical taste and behaviour can be found in Mark Tarrant, Adrian North & David Hargreaves (2002) 'Youth identity and music' (pp. 134–150) in Raymond MacDonald, David Hargreaves & Dorothy Miell (Eds.) *Musical Identities*. See also Dolf Zillmann and Su-lin Gan (1997) 'Musical taste in adolescence' (pp. 161–187) in David Hargreaves & Adrian North (Eds.) *The Social Psychology of Music*; and Adrian North & David Hargreaves (2008) *The Social and Applied Psychology of Music*.

music is acquired. Musical skills and attributes are particularly striking when they are developed disproportionately, as in the case of so-called 'musical savants', who typically display limited linguistic and social skills alongside high levels of musical expertise. Anecdotal accounts of such individuals have a long history, but it is only in recent years that more systematic studies of the skills demonstrated by musical savants have been carried out.

John Sloboda tested the musical recall ability of 'NP', an autistic savant pianist in his twenties, who was able to reproduce a tonal piano piece by Grieg (*Melodie* Opus 47 No. 3) almost perfectly within a few minutes of hearing it, making only small errors that were consistent with the conventions of the genre. NP was unable to perform a less conventionally tonal piece by Bartók with a similar level of recall, which led the researchers to conclude that his skills were dependent upon coding and storing tonal music according to its structural features. More broadly, the demonstration of the role that structural coding plays in NP's musical memory suggests that the same is true for non-savant musicians. This is confirmed by research on 'chunking', first observed in text reading as a process of recognizing and memorizing patterns rather than processing individual letters or words or, in the case of music, notes or chords. By recognizing commonplace chords or sequences of notes, expert music readers make educated guesses about what is coming next, matching what they expect with what they read and subsequently hear.

Derek Paravicini, a blind pianist with severe learning difficulties, has become well known for his improvising skills which, like NP's feats of memorization, rely on the retention of structural and stylistic knowledge of jazz and light classical music. Initially self-taught from the age of four, Paravicini's piano technique was at first chaotic: lacking a visual model of how to move around the keyboard, he found his own solutions, even using his elbows to stretch intervals that were beyond the reach of his hands. Weekly, then daily piano lessons enabled Paravicini to acquire a more conventional technique through physical demonstration and imitation, and so to develop the freedom to improvise in the jazz, light classical, and pop styles he most enjoyed.[14] Studies using neuroimaging techniques to monitor Paravicini's brain activity as he listens to music have demonstrated that his mental function in processing music is well above the average but is limited by his inability to articulate that understanding verbally: when played a series of fragments of Beethoven's *Moonlight* sonata and asked to identify those containing pitch errors, Paravicini's verbal responses were almost random whereas his brain activation showed fast and accurate discrimination of pitch errors.[15]

The biographies of these remarkable musicians reveal an obsessive engagement with music from an early age, supported by dedicated teachers who helped them to develop the technical skill needed to progress to an advanced level. Sloboda suggests that the unrestricted opportunities for practice, the fixed concentration that is typical of savant behaviour, and the absence of any socially inculcated fear of failure each accounts in part for the advanced skills acquired by these individuals. By this argument, NP's and Paravicini's musical learning is different in extent from that undertaken by all instrumentalists but is not substantially different in kind.[16]

8.4 **Are musicians' brains different?**

A growing body of neuroscientific research in the past two decades has reported evidence of changes to the function and structure of the brain as a result of the specific skills and tasks of musical performance. Most famously, the so-called 'Mozart Effect', discussed in Chapter 6, by

---

[14] Derek Paravicini's biography can be found on the Wisconsin Medical Society website (www.wisconsinmedicalsociety.org/savant_syndrome/savant_profiles/derek_paravicini) and also at http://www.derekparavicini.net. Adam Ockelford, who until recently combined his work as Paravicini's piano teacher with research and advisory roles at the Royal National Institute for Blind People, has documented Derek's development as a musician in the book *In the Key of Genius: The Extraordinary Life of Derek Paravicini* (2007).

[15] This experiment, carried out by Linda Pring at Goldsmith's College, University of London, featured in a British television documentary about music and autism: The Musical Genius (Channel 5, September 25, 2006).

[16] John Sloboda's work with NP is summarized in several chapters of his collection of essays *Exploring the Musical Mind* (2005).

which a short-term improvement in spatial intelligence (demonstrated by paper-folding tasks) was shown in participants who had listened to a Mozart piano sonata, prompted widespread media coverage of the idea that music can improve brain function and spatio-temporal reasoning. The reality is inevitably more complex, but there is a growing body of evidence that musical activity – and instrumental motor skills in particular – do have a lasting effect on the neural pathways in musicians' brains, in the same way that London taxi drivers have been found to have enlarged structures in the hippocampus as a result of memorizing the thousands of possible routes through London's streets that their training requires. The cliché 'use it or lose it' appears to have a strong element of truth, in that the reinforcement of musical skills through repeated practice does appear to cause a physical change in brain structure.

The particular demands of different musical instruments have been shown to have distinct effects on the brain. Pianists, for example, who use their right and left hands equally in playing, have more symmetrical left and right motor cortices, with increased activation in these areas appearing after as little as a 20 minutes' instruction. String players, on the other hand, who need particularly well-developed motor skills in their left hand (for fingering), have been shown to have a larger and more responsive right primary somatosensory cortex – the part of the brain that is most intimately involved with the left hand. In both cases, the effects are greater when instrumental lessons and practice were begun early in life, before the age of seven. However, another study of professional pianists showed decreased activation in the left and right cortices compared with those of a control group, appearing to demonstrate that highly developed musical motor skills result in greater efficiency of neural resources – playing on 'automatic pilot'.[17]

---

17 Recent literature on neuroscientific research in music is summarized by Donald Hodges (2006) 'The musical brain' (pp. 51–68) in Gary McPherson (Ed.) *The Child as Musician*, and John Flohr and Donald Hodges (2006) 'Music and neuroscience' (pp. 7–39) in Richard Colwell (Ed.) *MENC Handbook of Musical Cognition and Development*. See also overviews provided by Robert Zatorre and Isabelle Peretz in the *Annual Review of Psychology* (2005) and Peretz and Zatorre (Eds.) *The Cognitive Neuroscience of Music* (2003).

It is tempting to conclude that because musical activity has a permanent effect on brain function, starting to learn early, when the brain is at its most plastic, is essential for reaching full musical potential. Although it is true that the brain is most responsive to creating synaptic connections in the first decade of life, the idea that there is a 'critical period' for music learning, after which the acquisition of musical skills becomes impossible, holds little currency among neuroscientists. The brain remains adaptable and capable of learning into adulthood, and given sufficient motivation and practice, new musical experiences and challenges can be met at any stage of life. The rapidly developing findings of neuroscientific research on music need to be understood alongside the more substantial body of evidence relating to social, educational, and family influences in musical development.

8.5 **Measuring musical learning**

Ralph is aged eleven, and in his first week of secondary school. It is Thursday afternoon and he feels tired from the many new experiences of that week – but the first lesson after lunch is Music, and he has been looking forward to this. He used to enjoy the percussion time they had at primary school, where the teacher helped them to make up their own pieces of music, and he is hoping that his secondary school lessons will be similar. He is surprised, therefore, to find that the Music lesson starts with a test: the class is told to listen to the instructions given by a posh-sounding man on a tape recording – 'You are going to hear …' – what's that word? Cords? He starts writing his answers on the small piece of paper he has been given, feeling increasingly panicked about whether he is answering correctly, and what the consequences will be if he does not. Are these notes the same or different? The boy next to him appears to be putting 'different' for every question, which probably means that he will get about half of them right. Ralph wishes he had thought of that.

Ralph is doing the Bentley test, one of a number of test batteries designed to measure children's listening perception against age-related norms – and luckily, such unhappy and potentially demoralizing uses of this test are increasingly rare. Such tests were once widely used in British schools to monitor students' progress and determine selection for instrumental tuition, and indeed were the most obvious point of connection between music education and psychology for many years. The tests invented by Carl Seashore in 1938 and Arnold Bentley in 1966 were among those that sought to isolate and measure the various components of musical perception, including the recognition of chords, intervals, timing, and dynamics. Their manner of presentation reflected the educational values of the early twentieth century: very formal in style, and more concerned with achieving a measurable outcome than with creating a learning experience for the participating children. Later tests tried to counteract these problems, with Gene Simons' tests of 1976, for example, framing the questions as a 'musical game' and revealing the fallibility of the results through the instruction – 'If you do not know the answer, then guess'. The earlier tests appeared to offer the promise of educational rigour and a reliable measure of musical aptitude, drawing on developmental theories and evidence to determine whether children were above average and so worthy of additional tuition. In retrospect it is obvious that this approach was seriously flawed, but it was part of an educational culture of testing children and allocating resources according to their apparent potential – and finding an alternative approach brings its own challenges.

Confidence in tests of this kind has gradually dwindled, at least in British music education, as teachers have recognized both the unreliability of the tests as a predictor of musical achievement and the undesirability of labelling some children as 'musical' and so excluding others from available provision and experiences. In the psychology of music, similarly, there has been a move away from the compartmentalizing of musical behaviours of which these tests are symptomatic: the focus in the tests is entirely on aural skill, artificially removed from real-world musical contexts and reduced to the 'right or wrong' perception of musical components. Such an approach produces a rating of children's performance that gives a misleading impression of objectivity, ironing out the messiness of everyday musical behaviour in which researchers have more recently become interested.

Although hindsight clearly reveals the limitations of these tests as indicators of musical competence, the problems of assessing musical development remain of concern to instrumental and classroom music teachers. Some of these problems are conceptual: for instance, what does it mean to measure musical ability? There are so many elements to musicianship – rhythm and pitch processing, melodic recall, harmonic perception, sight-reading ability, motor skills on an instrument, and memorization – that choosing one or two to focus on (as the Seashore and Bentley tests did) gives higher value to some skills and overlooks important factors such as motivation, concentration, and other aspects of personality. There are practical difficulties in measuring ability too: is it possible to isolate specific aspects of musical skill, measure them reliably, and then use them as a predictor of general musical achievement? The 'yes' gets a little more uncertain at each stage. Nonetheless, parents, teachers, potential employers – and pupils themselves – are understandably keen to see evidence of progress in music, particularly in performance, where substantial investment of time and money has often taken place. It is hardly surprising, then, that the measurement of performing skills has a long history, even predating the inclusion of class music lessons in the British school curriculum. The founding of the Associated Board of the Royal Schools of Music (ABRSM) in the late nineteenth century marked the beginning of an examination system that would influence instrumental teaching across the world. Graded examinations were devised to assess the progress of students from the beginning level to advanced diplomas, setting a pattern of testing solo performance, sight-reading ability, scales, arpeggios, and aural skills that has shaped the instrumental learning of generations of children.

In the waiting room at the Associated Board examination centre, Clare (aged 9) sits nervously trying to remember the fingering for F major on her flute. She knew this last night, but today her hands feel sticky and she cannot remember whether there should be an E flat in the scale. Never mind, she knows her pieces will go well, and with luck the examiner will ask her to play other scales that feel more secure.

As she looks at the clock on the wall, a trumpeter a few years older than her comes back from his exam, looking confident and saying to his waiting granddad that the sight-reading was really easy. She hopes hers will be too, and tries that scale once more – 'F, G, A, B, no, B flat …'

Working towards exams can be a powerful motivator for some children, allowing them to measure their progress against their own previous achievement and that of their peer group. Nonetheless, the association of performance with critical evaluation and potential failure does little to prepare children for the experience of communicating with a concert audience, and can have the counterproductive effect of increasing anxiety and so lowering the motivation and confidence of some young players. Psychological research offers some explanations for why the same exam situation will act as a positive motivation for some children while severely damaging the confidence of others – a distinction explained through the contrast between 'adaptive' or 'mastery-oriented' motivational behaviour and 'maladaptive' or 'helpless' behaviour.

One experiment exposed children to a listening test in which they were told at various points that they had failed, and then asked to rate their confidence at succeeding in the next part of the test. Those with 'maladaptive' characteristics lost confidence and became less effective after experiencing failure – regardless of their previous success rate – whereas those with 'adaptive' characteristics seemed to view failure as part of the learning process, and to resume the task with renewed determination.[18] More generally, learners who attribute success to innate ability, rather than to effort or perseverance, have been shown to display 'helpless' characteristics, believing that no matter how hard they work, they will never improve at a task. In music exams, therefore, feedback and results will have quite different effects on students according to their learning strategies: for some, the outcome (whatever it is) will be taken as incidental to the learning process and will have little effect on confidence or application; for others, an unsuccessful experience will lead to loss

---

[18] For further details of this study, see Susan O'Neill and John Sloboda, 'The effects of failure on children's ability to perform a musical test' in *Psychology of Music* (1997).

of direction and self-belief. Children can be helped towards a greater focus on 'learning goals' rather than 'performing goals' in their musical practice and behaviour, such that they become less dependent on external rewards for their sense of achievement and enjoyment.

8.6 **Losing music**

Contemplating the age-related loss of musical faculties may seem a rather gloomy topic but is worth considering here, because the experiences of older listeners and participants shed new light on musical acquisition throughout the lifespan. Research in this area is relatively limited – perhaps because of the ethical sensitivities of addressing such potentially distressing topics through empirical investigations. Some studies exist that document the physical effects of ageing on the ability to listen and perform, but so far there has been little consideration of the emotional and psychological effects of music in later life.[19]

The ageing process brings with it a decline in hearing and motor dexterity, with significant consequences for those who have enjoyed listening to or performing music throughout their lives.[20] Professional musicians are somewhat protected from this decline in musical skill and accuracy, because the continuation of deliberate practice into late adulthood results in an expertise that helps to compensate for the effects of ageing. Amateur musicians may not be so fortunate, because they will have amassed fewer hours of focused practice over their lifetimes, with correspondingly weaker compensatory effects. Amateur singers, in particular, face the difficulties of coping with changing vocal apparatus, as the laryngeal cartilage gradually ossifies, with a subsequent loss of vocal range and flexibility. The 'warbling' tones of some older singers are the result of excessive vibrato caused by a loss of muscular stability,

---

[19] See the summary of musical development and ageing provided by Heiner Gembris in *MENC Handbook of Musical Cognition and Development* (2006, pp. 147–154); and in Gembris's edited book, *Musical Development from a Lifespan Perspective*, the chapter by Krampe (2006, pp. 91–105).

[20] In 2002, a special issue of *Psychomusicology* (Vol 18, No 1/2) focused on 'psychogeromusicology'. It was edited by Annabel Cohen and included papers on the cognitive and emotional functions of music in later life. Also relevant to this topic are Vernon Pickles' article on listening habits in later years – 'Music and the third age' (2003) and Carol Prickett's paper 'Music and the special challenges of aging: a new frontier' (1998).

although such physiological problems can be avoided through appropriate vocal exercises. Music is an area in which abilities can be preserved into advanced age, as witnessed by the notorious longevity of symphony orchestra conductors, found in one survey to have a mortality rate that was 38% lower than that of the general population.[21] However, similar results were found among top corporate executives, suggesting that the effect may have been related to job satisfaction and professional status rather than any specifically musical features of the conductors' lives.

The foundations for a secure musical old age are laid in childhood, as older adults are more likely to continue with long-valued activities than to take up new ones. Where habits of instrumental performance or concert attendance have already been established, these continue to provide a source of social interaction and well-being for those who pursue musical activities in late adulthood. Don Coffman writes movingly of the New Horizons Band that he conducts in Iowa City, where the average performer age is 71. He notes how the players support one another through ill health and bereavement, such that the band becomes a social lifeline as well as a source of musical satisfaction.[22] These qualities of musical participation are evident throughout the lifespan but are particularly striking in retirement, where opportunities to combine social interaction and personal expression become more scarce, and yet remain vital to a balanced and fulfilling life.

Early experiences of music also have a profound effect on shaping listening habits, because the music heard during a person's formative years will remain significant (although not necessarily liked) throughout the lifespan, acting as a kind of benchmark by which more recent music is evaluated. A survey of older listeners found evidence of stable but developing tastes, showing how musical preferences and concert attendance habits had been established much earlier in life. This 'imprinting' of

---

[21] For further discussion of music and longevity, see Barbro Johansson's 'Music, age, performance, and excellence: a neuroscientific approach' in *Psychomusicology* (2002).

[22] Don Coffman's work with the musicians he affectionately calls 'chronologically gifted' is reported in 'Banding together: new horizons in lifelong music making' (2002 : *Journal of Aging and Identity*). Similar experiences of the value of music in retirement are reported by interviewees in Terrence Hays and Victor Minichiello's study, ' The meaning of music in the lives of older people: a qualitative study' in *Psychology of Music* (2005).

musical generations has implications for music therapy, where the use of music that has strong personal significance is often particularly effective in triggering long-term memories and emotional responses. Research into musical development has tended to focus on the pre-adolescent years, but questions remain unanswered about the role of music in later life: to what extent does music sustain and secure self-identity as health, work, and family circumstances change in later years? And how could music be more effectively used to support the well-being of older people, whether as participants or as listeners? These are sensitive topics but could usefully contribute to a debate about the welfare of an increasingly ageing population.

Summary

This chapter has shown that the acquisition of musical skills is affected throughout the lifespan by biological and environmental factors, as physical and neurological development interacts with education, opportunity, and motivation to shape an individual's musical direction and identity. The research evidence for typical patterns of musical development, although considerable, is limited by the difficulties in reproducing 'real-world' musical behaviours in experimental conditions: in developmental research, the need to isolate musical components for accurate measurement, and in neurological research, the challenge of using often noisy neuroimaging equipment to capture the complexities of musical processing. Biographical research, looking at the characteristics of high achieving musicians, has identified parents, teachers, siblings, and friends as significant influences on acquiring musical interest and skill, and has demonstrated that large quantities of purposeful practice are essential to attaining mastery of a musical instrument. Between them, however, these various strands of research can offer only limited suggestions for identifying the critical factors involved in musical skill acquisition – let alone practical strategies for exploiting them optimally: musical development is an idiosyncratic process in which circumstances, opportunities, and motivation are different for everyone.

Chapter 9

Contexts for learning

9.1 Connecting music, education and psychology

Acquiring musical understanding and skill occurs in many contexts, from informal engagement with music in everyday life to the more structured approaches of classroom and instrumental lessons. Music educators and music psychologists are interested in similar questions about learning: how environmental factors influence children's attitudes, for example, or how musical behaviour in and out of school contributes to a young person's understanding of what it means to be 'a musician'. Parents, teachers, and students also have to think about these questions, framed in more practical ways. Why do some children appear to have an interest and aptitude for music while others do not? What are the effects and benefits of musical participation for young people? And what are the best ways to engage all children in musical activity, whatever their longer-term intentions and aspirations?

Consider how the following situation might be viewed by researchers and practitioners in education and psychology.

A group of four 12-year-olds are in the corner of their music classroom getting on with the task that they have been set by their teacher – to compose a piece for percussion using repeating rhythms. They have been working on their piece for about fifteen minutes, but their efforts are starting to fragment: Lizzie, a proficient violinist, is becoming frustrated by her attempts to notate the piece, while Liam and Daniel are loudly intent on reproducing the style of drumming they have recently seen on a pop video. The group is finding it hard to work together, and their fourth member, Caitlin, begins to organize them, acting as a conductor and telling the boys to be quiet.

It is easy to leap in with a 'teacherly' response, constrained by the formal educational context: it might seem that the girls are much more focused on the task and the boys are just messing around. But a more reflective approach, informed by the psychology of learning, reveals that all the students are drawing on experiences from outside the classroom, and are adapting the task to accommodate their individual views of musical performance. The attempt at notation, for example, draws on Lizzie's violin tuition, where learning music from a written score dominates her musical understanding. Liam and Daniel are using their informally acquired knowledge of musical style and exploring that through their playing. And Caitlin, who takes on the conducting role in an attempt to bring the group back together, clearly feels pressure to conform and complete the set task, which may be a reflection of her approach to school in general. A variety of learning approaches and musical behaviours are evident in this example, illustrating the scope for psychological investigation of children's developing musical expertise. However, in a conventional sense, the educational aims of the lesson are being lost in a way that many teachers, and certainly most teaching quality inspectors, would find unacceptable. This interpretation of a familiar classroom scene may not help to resolve its pressing educational dilemmas, but it could increase understanding of the ways in which children respond to music in schools, and how those classroom experiences connect with their wider musical learning.

The immediacy of classroom life ordinarily limits the potential for reflection on young people's musical behaviour, because it is rare for teachers to have the time to conduct systematic research into the learning experiences of their students. This is a pity, because better access to practitioners' detailed knowledge of what really goes on in music classrooms would help to connect theoretical perspectives with the pragmatic demands facing teachers. Similarly, although research into other aspects of musical behaviour has increasingly used 'real-world' approaches and settings, the classroom remains relatively uncharted research territory for music psychologists, perhaps because of its particular ethical and practical challenges. This disjunction of methods, findings, and contexts can disguise or distort the relevance of psychological research to classroom practice. The 'Mozart Effect' is a case in point (see Chapters 6 and 8): the media interpretation that music can 'make you smarter' has spawned a whole industry of musical toys and recordings designed to nourish the intelligence of the next generation[1]. Viewed in an optimistic light, it seems as though this research and the publicity surrounding it have secured a place for music within the school curriculum by drawing attention to its measurable benefits for child development. However, 'music', within neuroscientific research, often turns out to be narrowly constrained to passive listening, simple rhythm games, or brief periods of instrumental tuition – which form only a small part of the school music curriculum. The isolation of specific aspects of musical development makes good research sense but presents only a partial picture of what it means to acquire musical skill and understanding.

9.2 Reasons to acquire music

Throughout much of the twentieth century, school music education was explicitly seen as a source of knowledge and civilization that protected children from the degenerate influences of the jazz and, later, pop music that was becoming increasingly accessible with the advent of the gramophone and radio broadcasting. For decades, Western classical music dominated the curriculum, and the aims of music education were clearly defined: children should leave school with knowledge of the 'great' composers, and the ability to sing in tune and read notation[2]. The scope of musical education has rightly become much more contested, changing to accommodate wider access to different genres and traditions of music, and to reflect educational approaches that value independent thought and exploration above rote learning. School learning is therefore – in theory at least – now more compatible than

---

[1] For an example of the original reporting of the 'Mozart Effect' research, see Frances Rauscher *et al.*, (1993) 'Music and spatial task performance', in the journal *Nature*. For a popular media interpretation of such research and evidence of its marketing to parents and others, see Don Campbell's website http://www.mozarteffect.com

[2] Accounts of the historical development of British music education are given by Bernarr Rainbow and Gordon Cox (2006) *Music in Educational Thought and Practice*, and Stephanie Pitts (2000) *A Century of Change in Music Education*.

ever with the self-education in music that takes place whenever young people buy and listen to recorded music, compose independently using home computers, or rehearse in bands with their peers.

In many secondary schools in Britain, music thrives as much beyond the curriculum as within it, with opportunities for students to perform in choirs, orchestras, and other ensembles. In socio-economically disadvantaged school communities where such provision is lacking, educational outreach programmes can bring creative opportunities that raise the musical awareness and skills of young people with otherwise limited access to the arts. Other European countries offer more stratified music provision: students must opt to attend specialist music schools if they have aspirations as performers, whereas the general music education that is more widely available focuses mainly on listening and appreciation. The British educational emphasis on 'music for all' reflects the antipathy to artistic elitism which underpins the UK's thriving amateur musical culture, while also generating frequent public debate about the relevance of the arts for the population as a whole. This ambivalence towards music and its cultural value has strong educational implications: although it is generally accepted that music is a necessary ingredient in a truly comprehensive education, political enthusiasm and funding do not extend to giving all children long-term access to instrumental tuition, or to providing the increased staffing and smaller class sizes that would make a substantial difference to curriculum provision in music.

The content and style of school music teaching varies between countries but generally shares the broad aim of interesting and engaging students in musical activity. Variation in provision according to the interests of individual teachers might be assumed to have disappeared with the introduction of national curricula, but research consistently demonstrates the powerful influence of music teachers on their students' perceptions and experiences of the subject. Perhaps more than in other subjects, music teachers are closely identified with the subject they teach – being a 'musician' is part of being a music teacher – and they may therefore have a significant impact on their students' attitudes towards learning music. Surveys of student opinion over the past few decades have sometimes shown school music to be rather unpopular, but more recent research shows a change, perhaps reflecting the broadening of the curriculum to include repertoire and activities that relate more closely to students' out-of-school experiences.[3] Students surveyed in 2002 in England voiced their approval for many aspects of the contemporary music curriculum, including group composing, playing instruments, and meeting professional musicians, but had much less interest in learning abstract facts about music and musicians, and declined in their enthusiasm for singing after primary-school years. Music was felt to be a valuable part of the school culture, even among those students who did not participate in extra-curricular activities. The idea that music education is in a state of crisis appears to be an outdated one, but surveys of this kind show that students have high expectations and demands of their music lessons, and so the challenge remains for practitioners and researchers to identify and refine the successful elements of current classroom practice.

9.3 Acquiring music in the classroom

Music education has been increasingly drawn in to the broader debate about 'transferable skills' – those incidental aspects of learning that might occur as a result of engaging in musical activities but which are not concerned with the knowledge and skills of the subject itself. Group composition, for example – a common practice in many British classrooms – is often cited as providing a forum for cooperation, peer learning, and team work, although there is no empirical evidence that it achieves these ends any more effectively than, say, team sports or project work in geography. As group work is often expedient in making the best use of the available space, instrumental resources, and teacher time, research has concentrated on finding the most effective ways to

---

[3] Among the studies to show the relative unpopularity of music in the curriculum, the most recent and substantial is that conducted by the National Foundation for Educational Research, *Arts Education in Secondary Schools: Effects and Effectiveness* (2000). Alexandra Lamont, David Hargreaves, Nigel Marshall & Mark Tarrant present a more optimistic perspective in their 'Young people's music in and out of school' (2003), which features the 2002 survey described above.

make it work, considering mixed-sex groups versus single-sex groups or friendship groups versus ability grouping. Such investigations are valuable for informing classroom practice, allowing useful comparisons with other curriculum subjects, and so setting musical learning in its broader educational context, but there is also scope for questioning existing practices and looking for alternatives. Imagine a few moments in a typical secondary-school music classroom in England:

> Michelle has set her Year 8 (aged 12–13) students a composing task: 'work in pairs using the keyboards to produce a theme tune for a TV sports programme.' She goes round the classroom giving additional instructions, guidance, and encouragement where needed, and as she does so, she looks around the classroom to check that all the students are working. Michelle notes that most seem to be 'on task' but that some are engaged in chat that may not be work-related, and she calls out a five-minute warning, telling the students that they will shortly have to play their completed theme tunes to the rest of the class.

The student and teacher behaviours depicted here prompt a number of questions:

- What are the musical demands that are being made of these students?
- How do those demands relate to their previous musical learning and experience – which will vary widely across the class?
- What role is Michelle playing in their learning?
- What other strategies for learning might the students be drawing upon?
- How do the social requirements of the task interact with the musical ones?
- What different skills and attributes will be needed for the imminent performance to the rest of the class?

Teachers' and students' moment-by-moment responses to the questions implied by classroom practice usually go unarticulated, and are answered through actions based on prior experience and educational values. Indeed, it can be daunting to consider the full implications of some of these questions, because they reveal the complexity of teaching music to large groups of children with a wide range of musical interests and skills. Take the first question in the list above: Michelle may have information on the prior learning that has been experienced by this class; she might have taught them the previous year or at least know the curriculum they have followed, and is likely also to be aware of which children are taking additional instrumental lessons. But she is unlikely to know in any detail the kinds of music that the students choose to listen to at home or the extent to which they have heard and considered the conventions of sports broadcasting or television theme tunes more generally. She will know something of the behavioural tendencies of some of the class – at least the disruptive ones – but is less likely to have systematic information on their preferred learning strategies, their communication skills, and their personality types, all of which will have some effect on each child's response to the task.

Michelle's professional knowledge and experience allow her to manage the classroom effectively, such that she may appear to have no need for the more detailed investigations that systematic research might bring to bear upon a familiar situation. However, where such research has been carried out, it has had far-reaching implications for education. Patricia Shehan Campbell's ethnographic observations of children's everyday musical experiences makes uncomfortable reading for teachers, as Campbell analyses an apparently well-structured music lesson to find the children engaging in more complex musical behaviour when they are 'off-task' than during teacher-directed rhythm and singing activities.[4] The children's musical responses may deviate from the lesson plan, but they demonstrate the ways in which their capacities are more developed than could be revealed in the course of the teacher-led activities. Allowing children to explore their creative potential more freely often shows their implicit musical understanding – just as the

---

4 The account of 'Mrs Bedford's music class' can be found in Patricia Shehan Campbell's (1998) book, *Songs in Their Heads: Music and its Meaning in Children's Lives.*

idiosyncrasies of a young child acquiring language skills reveal their implicit but unstable knowledge of plurals, word order, and other grammatical conventions.

Returning to the example above, Michelle's role in the students' musical learning is of obvious interest to both practitioners and researchers, revealing as it does an implicit understanding of the ways in which musical skills are acquired and developed. Imagine that she stops to help one pair of students and finds that they have invented a two-bar opening phrase for their tune, but having played this repeatedly at different octaves on the keyboard, they have lost a sense of focus and begun to argue, interrupting one another with increasingly inaccurate playing of their short phrase and dismissing each other's ideas for how the piece should continue. As Michelle stops to help them, she might defuse the tension that is building up by praising the students' initial efforts and demonstrating ways in which they could extend their musical ideas to complete the task – playing the two-bar phrase backwards, perhaps, or picking out a smaller motif to repeat and develop. As a more experienced musician, she is 'scaffolding' their ideas[5] – showing them that they are already some way to solving the musical problem they are faced with, and providing them with new knowledge or strategies that build on their existing achievements. Elsewhere in the classroom, some pairs of students are able to fulfil this role independently, by pooling their musical expertise and learning from each other. Such cooperation is more likely to flourish when students are working in friendship groups and enjoying the task because, like other complex group tasks, composing together requires sophisticated communication skills and a sense of trust between the collaborators.

Acquiring music clearly involves much more than amassing historical or theoretical knowledge, or the motor skills of playing an instrument – although these elements of learning are demanding enough. Encounters with music also have an effect on attitudes and identity, with implications

---

5 'Scaffolding' is a term used in the educational theories of Lev Vygotsky to describe the role of the adult in supporting the child's learning by modelling and supporting strategies to take the child beyond his or her existing understanding into the 'zone of proximal development'. Summaries of the educational theories of Vygotsky, Piaget, and others can be found in David Wood (1988) *How Children Think and Learn*.

far beyond the classroom. In particular, school music can shape people's perceptions of the extent to which they consider themselves to be 'musical', often with lifelong implications for their subsequent involvement in musical activity. Some of the most vivid reported memories relate to extra-curricular musical activities: regular concert-goers recalling their experiences of performing with the school orchestra, music teachers choosing to invest hours in a school production so that their students can experience the same involvement that began their own musical career, or singer-songwriters tracing their regular semi-professional gigs back to the formation of a folk group at school.[6] Many music teachers are motivated by this feature of their chosen career, and life history studies have identified a point of crisis for middle-career teachers when it becomes apparent that promotion – which obviously has important career consequences – will take them away from the classroom, towards greater administrative responsibility and reduced contact with students.[7]

Although any peer group will inevitably include children with different levels of musical interest and achievement, the days of instructing some of the class (those considered to lack 'musicality') to stand at the back of the choir and mime are thankfully largely gone from education, helped by increasing evidence from psychological research that everyone has musical potential to some degree. School is only one among many factors that influence musical development, taking its place alongside parents, friendship groups, siblings, and the wider cultural environment. Nonetheless, the potential impact of classroom learning is

---

[6] Stephanie Pitts' book *Valuing Musical Participation* (2005a) includes examples of interviews with audience members at the Music in the Round Chamber festival, also discussed in her (2005) article 'What makes an audience? Investigating the roles and experiences of listeners at a chamber music'. For a case study of extracurricular music making, see Pitts (2007) '*Anything Goes:* A case study of extra-curricular musical participation in an English secondary school'.

[7] The following journal articles from the *British Journal of Music Education* focus on the professional lives and identities of music teachers: Brendan Drummond (2001) 'The classroom music teacher – inspirations, aspirations and realities. The evidence from Northern Ireland'; David Baker (2005) 'Peripatetic music teachers approaching mid-career: a cause for concern?'; and from *Music Education Research*, Gordon Cox (1999) 'Secondary school teachers talking'.

vast, in shaping later attitudes and in providing formative opportunities to engage with musical materials.

9.4 Acquiring instrumental skills

There are many points of connection between formal and informal learning, and between the environments of home and school, demonstrated most clearly in the various ways in which people acquire performing skills. Although approaches to instrumental teaching are culturally specific, the notion of an apprentice receiving tuition from an expert is found across a wide range of cultural contexts. Sometimes this process is relatively indirect and might be better described as 'enculturation', with the learner picking up instrumental skills from more proficient players in a relatively haphazard and opportunistic manner. At other times it is more systematic, such as when large groups of young people are taught principally through band rehearsals rather than individual lessons, as in some North American and Australian schools. Methods in British schools, and in the private lessons that take place in teachers' or students' homes, are typically more structured: individual or small group lessons take place for a fixed duration, usually once a week, and learning is supported through individual practice between lessons.

Learning a musical instrument makes distinctive demands of students, who must set aside time for the independent practice of repetitive and often difficult physical and cognitive tasks. As their physical skills become more refined, they will also need to engage with the more subjective realms of performance expression and interpretation in preparation for the possibly daunting task of playing in front of an audience. Few children who decide to play an instrument are aware of these impending demands and commitments: if they were, there would probably be far fewer volunteers for instrumental lessons than the already small proportion of the school-age population receiving tuition.

One attempt to investigate young people's attitudes to instrumental learning involved around 150 young instrumental beginners in Sydney, Australia, who participated in a three-year study. These children were asked to give their reasons for learning and to predict the length of time they would continue with the instrument, and their intentions were found to correspond closely to their actual behaviour as learners. Those who intended to play only until they moved into secondary education (at the age of 11), or who were influenced by extrinsic factors such as the prospect of a group outing to a burger bar after concerts, tended to make the least progress, regardless of the quantity of practice they did. Children who had high intrinsic motivation and longer-term ambitions for themselves as instrumentalists generally coupled this with greater commitment to practice, and so made more significant progress in their first nine months of study.[8] Parents who have musical ambitions for their children might agonize over the optimum time to begin learning, but a far more important variable is the amount of interest, enthusiasm, and commitment shown by beginner instrumentalists, and the extent of the support that will be given by their families.

Seven-year-old Emma is offered instrumental lessons at school, and with support from her parents decides to take up a woodwind instrument. She rejects the flute on the grounds that, based on her experience of playing the recorder, an instrument where you cannot see your fingers as you play seems too difficult. A friend's older sister plays the oboe and presents an appealing role model, but Emma ends up learning the clarinet because the family is able to borrow one from a relative.

Emma's experience illustrates the often arbitrary or compromised decisions that begin the process of acquiring musical skills. For the

---

[8] This project, led by Gary McPherson and Jane Davidson and funded by an Australian Research Council grant, traced the experiences of beginning instrumentalists in their first three years of learning. Articles resulting from the project include a paper in *Music Education Research* by Stephanie Pitts, Jane Davidson & Gary McPherson (2000) 'Developing effective practice strategies: case studies of three young instrumentalists', in which video data of three children's practice sessions are analysed. A summary of the project is provided by Gary McPherson in 'From child to musician: skill development during the beginning stages of learning an instrument' published in *Psychology of Music* (2005).

children in the Australian study mentioned earlier, similarly diverse factors affected their choice of instrument: they might have seen older siblings or friends playing in the school band and wanted to join in, but they were just as likely to want to play 'a nice heavy instrument so you get muscles and stuff carrying it around' – as one of the participants put it. Given the rarity of subsidized instrumental lessons in schools, factors such as home socio-economic context and parental support often limit the instrumental choice available to many children, perpetuating the tendency for classical music performance to be the preserve of relatively affluent families. Research on instrumental learning has inevitably concentrated on those who have been given such opportunities, and there are questions with broad social ramifications for those children and families whose attitudes to musical performance are shaped by a lack of access at this early stage.

Playing a musical instrument can offer an immediate sense of achievement for beginners, as they experience the unfamiliar pleasures of getting first a sound and then a recognizable tune from their instrument. After these initial strides in learning, however, comes the realization that sustained effort is necessary to continue making progress, and here the extent of a child's determination to persevere and succeed will start to have significant effects on the rate of learning. Transforming initial, extrinsic motivators to practise into more sustainable, intrinsic drives is vital as a young instrumentalist becomes increasingly self-governing in the desire to practise and develop performing skills. The question remains why some children practise and others do not – a difference that has been attributed to factors including the personality of the child, expectations of influential adults, and practical circumstances of the home environment. Practice is an isolating activity, demanding concentration and perseverance, so it is no surprise that – as pointed out in Chapter 7 – personality studies have shown musicians as a group to be relatively introverted, able therefore to focus on activities requiring a high degree of repetition and commitment. At their most well-adjusted, musicians are characterized as 'bold introverts', who can transform their hours of solitary practice into a performance and feel comfortable in both the private and the public environments.[9] It is almost impossible to disentangle the causality here, and to determine whether these personality types are drawn to musical activity, or whether the reverse is true: years of practice can turn a potential extrovert into a 'bold introvert'. Parents anxious about shaping their child's personality by sending them to instrumental lessons might be reassured to know that musicians are also characterized as being self-sufficient, imaginative, and sensitive (although no doubt all readers will be able to think of exceptions among the musicians of their acquaintance).

Parents and teachers can significantly influence effective practice habits, although praising the repetitive, persistent practice of a difficult phrase as well as the fluent reading of a well-known piece can be hard for even the most understanding parents. It is vital, however, that such sources of praise are not the child's principal motivation to practise, because the desire to please other people, or to earn rewards associated with practice, is not sufficient to sustain long-term commitment to learning. Giving up instrumental playing and learning is particularly common among secondary-school students – as in the first example below. Faced with ever-increasing amounts of homework and assessment, learning an instrument can feel like an additional chore for all but the most dedicated students. When the less determined withdraw from musical activities, the divide between 'musicians' and 'non-musicians' (to use a widespread but problematic term) is reinforced in ways that persist into adulthood, as lapsed performers look back with regret at the opportunities they gave up as children. Starting to learn an instrument as an adult appears to be so much harder, not only because of the greater difficulties of acquiring the necessary cognitive and motor skills but also because the support networks of peer learners, school and county ensembles, and readily accessible teachers are designed with the school-aged beginner in mind. For learners of all ages, there are competing interests and pressures against which opportunities for practice, and commitment to instrumental learning, must be weighed.

[9] See Anthony Kemp's work on the personality of musicians: *The Musical Temperament: Psychology and Personality of Musicians* (1996).

Amir has learned the violin since primary school but decides at the age of 14 to give up his lessons. He is being pressured by teachers to concentrate on his curriculum subjects and has recently started to feel that having to practise at home is a bit too much like having extra homework. Amir misses his participation in the school orchestra – but not the teasing of his peers that he had to endure whenever he carried his instrument case on the school bus.

Shortly after her fiftieth birthday, Morag decides to overcome memories of unhappy piano lessons as a child by taking up the fiddle, joining a friend who plays in weekly pub sessions in her home city of Aberdeen. She practises several times a week between sessions, learning new tunes by ear from a CD and playing the tunes from the last session more slowly with the systematic aim of improving her instrumental technique. Fitting in practice time among the other demands of her life is tricky but made worthwhile by the musical and social pleasure of playing traditional music among friends.[10]

Research on instrumental learning has often been explicitly concerned with finding the most efficient and effective ways to acquire advanced musical expertise. Individual practice is often at the core of such investigations, and the researchers who found that expert performers had amassed around 10,000 hours of practice by the age of 21 have no doubt been frequently quoted by informed instrumental teachers wanting to persuade their pupils to work harder.[11] However, this focus on traditional

---

[10] The example of the Scottish fiddler is influenced by Peter Cope's studies of amateur music making in the Scottish folk world, including his article 'Adult learning in traditional music' (2005). Jonathan Stock presents comparable investigations of learning within English folk music traditions in his article in *World of Music*, 'Ordering performance, leading people: structuring an English folk music session' (2004) and in a chapter in *Empirical Musicology*, edited by Eric Clarke and Nicholas Cook (2004).

[11] The figure of 10,000 hours of practice comes from Ericsson, Krampe and Tesch-Römer's study of German violin students : 'The role of deliberate practice in the acquisition of expert performance' in *Psychological Review* (1993). Complementary evidence on the effort needed to acquire professional levels of musical expertise can be found in the work

routes towards the high-level performance of classical music somewhat distorts the picture of instrumental learning activity in contemporary Britain. As the example of Morag's fiddle playing illustrates, the acquisition of instrumental skill can flourish in diverse contexts, and need not necessarily involve the presence of a teacher or the delayed gratification of waiting to be 'good enough' to perform. Similar approaches to learning have been observed among pop musicians, jazz players, and world-music ensembles, where group music-making is at the heart of learning from the outset, and peer support and guidance replaces formal teaching.[12] The learning strategies of teenagers in pop groups, for example, include listening to and copying existing recordings of the music they play, rather than being dependent on notation or teacher instruction to define their musical goals. As well as challenging many educational assumptions, these informal learning practices shed new light on psychological questions of motivation, identity, and social interaction, challenging researchers to look beyond the classroom or instrumental lesson for their interpretations of what it means to be a young musician.

In her study of popular musicians and their learning strategies, Lucy Green illustrates the high levels of motivation and independence among young performers who acquire their musical expertise through playing in groups and listening to recordings. She suggests that the absence of formal tuition may have long-term effects on these musicians, who by virtue of their intrinsic drive to perform are more likely to continue with musical activities after leaving school. And the converse seems intuitively to be true – students who rely on an instrumental or school music teacher for the provision of opportunities and encouragement are ill equipped

---

of Maria Manturszewska, who notes that the early formation of a strong musical identity is also vital to performing success: see 'A biographical study of the life-span development of professional musicians' in *Psychology of Music* (1990).

[12] Lucy Green's book *How Popular Musicians Learn* (2001) presents interview data from pop musicians reflecting on their learning practices, which feature a greater degree of 'purposive listening' (listening and copying from a recording) and group collaboration than is typical of classical instrumental training. In jazz, David Sudnow has documented similar processes involved in learning to improvise at the piano (*Ways of the Hand*, 2001).

to continue their music making once those external sources of support have ceased. The initiative shown from the outset by a young musician engaged in informal learning is perhaps a stronger predictor of long-term involvement than the willingness to turn up for weekly piano lessons. One-to-one tuition has long been assumed to be the most direct route to acquiring musical proficiency, but the growing awareness of alternatives prompts a reappraisal of how instrumental teaching fosters particular habits and attitudes, which have their drawbacks as well as benefits.

9.5 **The consequences of acquiring music**

Acquiring music involves much more than gaining knowledge and expertise: it makes a contribution to identity and self-perception, which is only just beginning to be investigated and understood. As we saw in Chapter 7, even the term 'musician' has different meanings according to the context in which it is used and so reveals some of the value judge-ments and cultural assumptions that surround musical behaviour. Consider the extent to which the following people might be comfortable calling themselves 'musicians':

> Christine is 62 and a longstanding member of the Philharmonic Chorus in the city where she lives. She attends weekly rehearsals and participates in regular concerts of large-scale classical choral reper-toire, enjoying the experience of getting to know pieces of music in detail and being part of a full and impressive musical sound. She discovered her enjoyment of singing while at school but has never had individual lessons or learned to play a musical instrument.

> Charlie, aged 16, plays bass guitar in a band with friends and writes some of their music. The band meets regularly after school, using a room in the school music department provided by their teacher, who supports but does not contribute directly to their music making. The band has only played a couple of gigs so far but already has hopes for securing a record deal and making a living from playing.

Rebecca is a university music student, entering the final year of her degree course and facing decisions about her future career. She had hoped to be a professional performer but was disappointed not to get into the university orchestra this year (there was a glut of highly qualified flautists auditioning), and so has begun to doubt her own abilities. She is considering spending a few years as an instrumental teacher when she graduates, before applying for a postgraduate performing course.

If any of these musically active people were to describe themselves as 'musicians', it is likely that their use of the word would be hedged around with conditions and qualifiers, comparing themselves with other people and feeling excluded by the criteria associated with professional musical status. Investigations in and out of educational contexts have shown that people in diverse circumstances are often reluctant to declare a musical identity, even though musical involvement might be an integrated and essential part of their lives. Students in higher education question their entitlement to call themselves 'musicians' when, possibly for the first time in their educational careers, they are surrounded by peers with similarly high levels of skill and their place in the orchestra is no longer assured. Adults participating in performing groups or practising independently often doubt their status as musicians because they are not professionals, despite sustaining active performing lives at an amateur level, often to high standards. Musical identities appear to be relatively fragile, needing sustenance from regular musical activity and achievement, and from the affirmation that results from this: applause after a concert, the request to perform for a particular occasion, and the promise of future success and recognition.

Case study research with performing groups and audience members has illustrated the impact on people's lives of regular musical participation with like-minded enthusiasts.[13] Their experiences show how friendships, social networks, and a sense of belonging can be found

---

[13] Further discussion of musical participation and its effects on participants' lives and identities can be found in Stephanie Pitts' *Valuing Musical Participation* (2005).

through musical activities: participants are able to explore aspects of their own personality that might not have a role in other areas of their lives; they develop new skills or hone existing ones, and grow in confidence at using them in front of their peers and audiences; and they nurture their love of music through deliberate engagement with genres that appeal to them and are consistent with their broader outlook on life.

The performers' experiences illustrated above also reveal some of the costs of musical participation – not just the financial ones associated with travelling to rehearsals, buying concert tickets, or paying fees to attend a residential course, but also in terms of the emotional energy expended in preparing for a performance, not to mention coping with the sudden loss of focus when a musical event is over and the sense of guilt that might be felt over spending time away from families and other commitments. Many people struggle when asked to summarize the contribution that music makes to their lives, and resort to comparisons with alternative activities – football or acting, say – before asserting a preference for music as fulfilling their need for what some researchers have termed 'serious leisure'.[14] The role of music in the lives of those who participate regularly may be hard to describe, but it is undoubtedly significant in strengthening their well-being and sense of self, as well as providing opportunities to increase their musical knowledge, expertise, and interest.

For many adults, the principal musical activity in their lives is listening, an activity so widespread that the musical skills and awareness it involves can easily be overlooked. As discussed in Chapter 6, recent research has considered the ways in which people manipulate their moods (and those of other people) by incorporating music listening into their everyday lives. In doing so, they draw on their knowledge of repertoire and understanding of musical affect – expertise that may have been acquired in part through formal education but probably more through

---

[14] Robert Stebbins has written extensively on leisure, theorizing about concepts of 'casual' and 'serious' leisure, and conducting case studies of amateurs and 'hobbyists' across a range of activities. For work most directly relevant to music, see his book *The Barbershop Singer: Inside the Social World of a Musical Hobby* (1996), and for discussion of amateurism and serious leisure, see *Amateurs, Professionals, and Serious Leisure* (1992).

the informal exchange of musical tastes with friends and the exposure to musical mood-management through the background music encountered in shops, airports, and other public places.[15] Nick Hornby has written both fictional and autobiographical accounts that illustrate the strong identification with particular pieces of music that can result from everyday listening. He suggests that music acquires a personal significance, not through a single moment of discovery but through long association and repeated listening, during which the listener will solve the 'emotional puzzlement' that made the music initially attractive while remaining sufficiently interested in the music to want to hear it again.[16] The musical skills and interests of Hornby and millions of similarly committed listeners would not conventionally be described as musical participation, but they certainly contribute greatly to a sense of well-being and individual expression. Film and television audiences demonstrate finely tuned listening skills as they anticipate and interpret dramatic events through the musical clues provided in the soundtrack. Some writers have expressed concern that the ubiquity of music is damaging the ability to engage in focused listening, but it seems more likely that contemporary listeners are constantly transforming and adding to their skills in using music in daily life, developing new sensitivities, and adapting their responses to music.[17]

---

15 Tia DeNora's book *Music in Everyday Life* (2000) includes a discussion of mood regulation through music listening, as does Michael Bull's study, *Sounding Out the City: Personal Stereos and the Management of Everyday Life* (2000) and a follow-up accommodating changes in technology and music consumption habits, *Sound Moves: iPod Culture and Urban Experience* (2007). An entertaining history of Muzak is offered by Joseph Lanza in *Elevator Music* (2004).

16 Nick Hornby's ideas on music listening feature in his novel, *High Fidelity* (1995) as well as in *31 Songs* (2003), a book of brief essays on songs of personal significance. His views on the 'emotional puzzlement' of music listening coincide with those of D. E. Berlyne, who in *Aesthetics and Psychobiology* (1971) proposed an inverted-U relationship between familiarity and liking.

17 Julian Johnson and Simon Frith offer opposing arguments on this topic, with Johnson's *Who Needs Classical Music?* (2002) suggesting that the value of classical music is being eroded in contemporary society and Frith, in 'Music and everyday life' (2003) arguing that contemporary practices are in fact generating new listening skills, including those needed to interpret the soundtrack of a film.

Summary

This chapter has shown how formative experiences of music – acquired through formal education or otherwise – are the first step in lifelong engagement, and may shape young people's sense of the extent and manner in which they can behave 'musically' as adults. The examples discussed are embedded in Western educational and social values, reflecting the bias of existing research in music psychology and education – but a much greater variety of attitudes towards musical participation can be found around the world. The hierarchical separation of the professional, the amateur, and the 'non-musician', for instance, is dependent on the cultural notion of 'talent' as an attribute possessed by some and not others. The teaching and learning contexts examined here have sometimes highlighted differences between educational and psychological perspectives, but there is clearly great potential for the two disciplines to become more connected through their shared concerns with how musical development can be influenced and nurtured.

There are many remaining questions about musical learning and its contexts to which music psychology could make a contribution. For instance, the relationships between various influences on musical development, from home, school, media, and culture, are constantly changing and their effect on what it means to acquire music have yet to be thoroughly investigated. Teachers in traditional contexts are intuitively negotiating new roles that accommodate their students' increased autonomy as listeners, recognizing that 'school music' needs to be connected to the wider musical world that young people experience. Greater insight on the perceptions and behaviours of both teachers and students in such contexts would be helpful in reframing music education, ensuring that its methods and aims are flexible enough to keep pace with technological change, while providing a secure foundation for future musical involvement.

Chapter 10

The psychology of music – an overview

So far, in this book, we have presented an account of how music relates to people's experiences and behaviour in reasonably familiar and recognizable everyday circumstances. Since the aim of this book has been to explore and try to understand the nature of 'everyday music psychology', it has concentrated on questions and phenomena that are relevant to that aim, rather than focusing on those areas of published research that have been the most productive or controversial. In other words, we have not tried to reflect on the psychology of music as a discipline in either the structure of this book or the relative depth and extent of treatment that is allocated to different topics. But the psychology of music has become a well-established discipline, with its own institutions, publications, research agendas, and methods. The purpose of this last chapter is to give a critical overview of how music psychology has evolved as a field of research, the questions with which it has primarily been concerned, and the approaches that it has adopted.

10.1 **A short history**

Writings about the relationship between music and human behaviour go back to classical antiquity – in a broad sense, the psychology of music therefore has a very long history. The Greek philosophers Aristoxenus, Plato, and Aristotle all made important contributions to an understanding of the nature of musical materials and their effects on people, and were very aware of the power of music both to cause psychological and social unrest and to calm, soothe, divert, or give pleasure.[1] A number

---

[1] A wide-ranging collection of writings on music, from Greek antiquity to the end of the twentieth century, can be found in Oliver Strunk and Leo Treitler's *Source Readings in*

of fundamental principles that continue to influence the psychology of music in the 21st century were first established in those early writings (for better or worse), including ideas about music and mathematics, the emotional effects of different harmonic and melodic devices, the relationship between rhythm and motion, and the precursors of what has now become music therapy.

Important though these writings are from a historical perspective and in their continuing influence on contemporary psychology of music, the 'modern' psychology of music really dates from the rise of psychology itself, in the second half of the nineteenth century. The two most influential figures in early music psychology were Hermann von Helmholtz and Carl Stumpf, representing very different theoretical positions but both focusing principally on what might be called 'the elements of music': the sensations of pitch, rhythm, intensity, and timbre. This might be seen as both reasonable and ideologically loaded: reasonable because there is logic in looking at what might be thought of as the building blocks of music (pitches and rhythms) as the first step, but ideologically loaded in that this first move immediately positions music as an *object*, separated from human activity and divorced from its context. Helmholtz's and Stumpf's approaches were the forerunners of what is now known as *psychoacoustics*, the study of relationships between acoustical events (frequencies, durations, and intensities) and their physiological and psychological counterparts (pitches, timbres, rhythms, and loudness).

Helmholtz was an experimental psychologist, committed to the idea that an understanding of the physics of sound could be combined with an understanding of the physiology of the auditory system to provide an explanation of music and musical experience. His account of consonance and dissonance, for example, depended on the idea that the patterns of vibration in the inner ear, created by dissonant combinations of sounds, produced interference patterns that were perceived as a quality of beating or roughness. A physical attribute (the frequencies of the

Music History (1998). Specifically, Greek writing on music can be found collected in two volumes edited by Andrew Barker (1989).

components of two or more notes) is directly related to a physiological attribute (a pattern of vibration on the basilar membrane of the inner ear) that results in a perceptual experience (consonance or dissonance). From these physical and physiological principles, Helmholtz ultimately hoped to give an empirically-based scientific account of musical aesthetics.

Stumpf was also interested in using experimental findings but was committed to the primacy of human experience, and was in this sense anti-reductionist in outlook. He too developed a theory of consonance and dissonance, which not only took account of acoustical theory but also prioritized the intuitions and reported experiences of expert musicians.[2] An accomplished musician himself, he was acutely aware both of the highly differentiated perceptual sensitivities that musicians may develop and of the significant effects of local and wider context on people's musical judgements – an attitude that is difficult to reconcile with Helmholtz's more 'physicalist' outlook. Stumpf's sensitivity to the impact of context stimulated a much broader interest in the music of other cultures than was typical for many of his contemporaries, and he is credited with being the German founder of ethnomusicology. In many ways, Helmholtz and Stumpf represent two different approaches to music psychology, which are still apparent more than a century later: Helmholtz represents the attraction of an empirical scientific approach, whose aim is to explain the complexity of human musical experience in terms of a linked chain of physical, physiological, and psychological mechanisms; Stumpf represents the tradition that argues for the irreducibility of human experience, open to systematic investigation but thoroughly embedded in its social and cultural context.

After the work of Helmholtz and Stumpf, research in music psychology certainly did not cease altogether, but the trickle of publications from 1900 to the late 1960s remained disparate in both subject matter and

---

2 Some of Stumpf's most significant students were Edmund Husserl, the founder of phenomenology; and Max Wertheimer, Wolfgang Köhler, and Kurt Koffka – the founders of Gestalt psychology. The significance of these two legacies is that they emphasize Stumpf's anti-reductionist approach: human experiences cannot be reduced to a simple aggregation of primary sensations.

approach, with the consequence that a coherent field or discipline never really took shape. In his introductory chapter to the second edition of the *Handbook of Music Psychology*, Charles Eagle (1996) presents a chronological table of textbooks in music psychology published over the period from 1862 (when Helmholtz published his book *On the Sensations of Tone*) to 1996 (the date of Eagle's survey), showing that an average of about one book per year was published from 1920 to 1970, covering topics that range across music and communication, the nature of a musical prodigy, musical tests and measurement, music and maths, scientific approaches to the aesthetics of music, and much more. The exception to this very heterogeneous picture is the research carried out by Carl Seashore at the University of Iowa in the 1920s and 1930s. Seashore's principal achievement was to develop and exploit new ways to study musical performance with a detail and precision that had never been possible before. Up until the publication of this important body of research,[3] the majority of music psychology had been concerned with musical testing and aptitude or with laboratory studies of listening using highly simplified materials. Seashore's great contribution was to investigate performance rather than perception, and to do so (at least in some circumstances) using complex and sophisticated materials played by expert musicians. In these respects, Seashore was significantly ahead of his time, and it was not until around 1980 that this level of musical and technical sophistication was revived and developed (see below).

Mainstream psychology went through what some have characterized as the 'dark ages of behaviourism' from the 1920s to the early 1960s, during which time (at least in Anglophone psychology) there was an intense concentration on the observable *behaviour* of humans and other animals and a resistance to theorizing about what might be going on in the minds of those organisms. With the work of the linguist Noam Chomsky, and a growing number of psychologists on whom Chomsky's work had a dramatic influence, came the 'cognitive revolution' – a radical change in psychology in which the emphasis turned emphatically

---

[3] A summarizing overview of much of Carl Seashore's work can be found in his book *Psychology of Music* (1938/1967).

away from behaviour and inwards towards the mental processes and internal representations that might be inferred from the outward capacities of human subjects. The connection with language (through Chomsky's work) is significant: language is a distinctively human capacity that is endlessly creative, and yet clearly rule-governed – as shown by native speakers' sensitivities to 'unacceptable' utterances. You do not have to be a trained linguist to know that there is something wrong with the utterance 'Green furiously ideas sleep colourless', while 'Colourless green ideas sleep furiously' – although strange in terms of its meaning – is perfectly acceptable as a grammatical sentence.[4]

In simplified terms, Chomsky's approach to language was to assert that linguistic competence must be understood as the expression of a small number of powerful grammatical rules that constrain the otherwise infinite possibilities of a language and, at the same time, permit an indefinite number of new utterances to be created. Chomsky's theory quickly became immensely influential in linguistics, and was also adopted by many psychologists who saw the possibility to extend this principle beyond language into many other aspects of human behaviour. Suddenly a rule-based approach seemed to offer a powerful way to understand vision, motor skills, memory, creativity – and music.

Like language, music seems to be infinitely creative and yet highly structured, and just as Chomsky proposed that people's use and understanding of language could be explained by what he called a generative grammar (a finite set of rules that could generate an infinite number of different utterances that would all be comprehensible to someone who had internalized that set of rules), so others saw this as a way to understand how a competent listener could make sense of a completely new piece of music – as long as it was in a familiar style. Musical style is like a language, and the piece is like a new utterance – quite

---

4 Chomsky famously coined this 'semantically anomalous' sentence in order to point out the distinction between syntax and semantics: 'Colourless green ideas sleep furiously' is syntactically correct (try substituting 'bright' for 'colourless', 'lizards' for 'ideas', and 'peacefully' for 'furiously' and you will arrive at a perfectly straightforward sentence) but semantically contradictory (Colourless and green? An idea that is coloured? An idea that sleeps? Sleep that is furious?), whereas 'Green furiously ideas sleep colourless' is little more than an arbitrary jumble of words.

possibly a sequence of sounds that has never been encountered before but using principles that are very familiar from many other instances. This seemed to be a very powerful way to understand all kinds of phenomena in music psychology: melodies that are easy to remember conform to a readily identifiable pattern or 'grammar'; music that is interesting and emotionally engaging is constructed using a rule-governed system, but does not simply adhere slavishly to those rules, thereby arousing but not always confirming a listener's expectations; and expressive playing can be understood as a performer's systematic, but not entirely predictable, use of some simple rules relating musical structure to expressive gestures and transformations.

Around 1980, there began a dramatic increase in the productivity, profile, and wider acceptance of music psychology. The journal *Psychology of Music*, which aimed to cover both the psychology of music and music education,[5] was founded in 1973, but it is from the late 1970s that the discipline really took off. In a period of about eight years *The Psychology of Music* (Davies, 1978), the *Handbook of Music Psychology* (Hodges, 1980), *The Psychology of Music* (Deutsch, 1982), *Music, Mind and Brain* (Clynes, 1982), *A Generative Theory of Tonal Music* (Lerdahl and Jackendoff, 1983), *The Musical Mind* (Sloboda, 1985), *The Developmental Psychology of Music* (Hargreaves, 1986) as well as quite a number of other books were all published, and the journals *Music Perception* and *Psychomusicology* were founded. The strong emphasis in the great majority of the work published at this time (and which remains a dominating theme) was on the relationship between musical structure and psychological processes, most obviously expressed in the title (and contents) of the edited book *Musical Structure and Cognition* (Howell et al., 1985). The fundamental question that this stream of research addressed was how listeners perceive, remember, evaluate and distinguish between different musical sequences; and the primary theoretical framework took the idea of mental representations of musical structures as its central principle.

---

5 The journal was the product of the Society for Research in Psychology of Music and Music Education (SRPMME), subsequently renamed SEMPRE (Society for Education Music and Psychology Research).

In order to understand this approach, consider the following example: do listeners find it easier to remember tonal melodies than atonal melodies; and if so, why? The way in which this kind of question is often researched in the standard literature is to construct a series of melodies that differ in tonality while keeping other properties the same – such as rhythm, register, the average size of the intervals between adjacent notes, tempo, and so on. The melodies might then be played to a group of listeners who are tested for the accuracy of their memory in one way or another: they might be asked to try to sing back each melody as soon as they have heard it, or to judge whether a new comparison melody is the same as or different from the melody that they originally heard. Typically, what is found is that melodies with more conventional tonal structures are remembered better and that the kinds of mistakes that people make in trying to recall or recognize the original melodies demonstrate the influence of an internal, mental representation of the structure of the music. For instance, a melody that started with three notes from an A minor triad in the order E, A, C might be 'misremembered' as three notes from an E major triad (E, G#, B). This can be interpreted as the listener having heard and remembered that the melody starts with a triad but misremembering which triad it was and in which inversion, rather than just producing any arbitrary set of three notes positioned relatively close to one another. In other words, the explanation might be that in listening to a melody what a listener is trying to do is to establish the pattern of the melody, and that this pattern is then stored in some relatively stable and simple form. When it comes to either reproducing the melody or judging whether another melody is the same or different, the listener uses this stored representation as the basis for either producing a sung melody or making a comparison.

In this imaginary example, the key to understanding what listeners remember, and the kinds of mistakes that they make, is presented as a function of the kind of internal representation that they form. As a consequence, the research question becomes transformed into a search for the most appropriate, powerful, or plausible model of the listener's internal representation, based on the kinds of external evidence for the tunes that they find easy or difficult to remember and the patterns of mistakes that they make (if there *is* a pattern) in laboratory studies. Research from the 1980s is dominated by proposals for the kinds of models that might explain listeners' behaviour, using geometrical, mathematical, computational, and rule-system approaches. In 1992, John Sloboda wrote a review of what he regarded as the most influential published research in the psychology of music in the period 1980–1990 focusing mainly on the leading journal *Music Perception*.[6] Overwhelmingly, the most influential publications were concerned with representations of musical structure, all of them based around some kind of hierarchical arrangement (that is, organized according to a series of levels) and presented in more or less formalized terms. Foremost among these models was Fred Lerdahl and Ray Jackendoff's *A Generative Theory of Tonal Music* – a book-length study of the ways in which the perceptions and intuitions of experienced listeners to tonal music might be understood by means of an explicit cognitive rule system. John Sloboda had already identified this publication as the definitive moment when the psychology of music 'came of age',[7] because it provided for the first time a musically sophisticated as well as explicit and predictive model from which to generate empirical research questions: in short, it represented the basis for a whole array of definite and testable hypotheses that could be pursued by means of well-established scientific methods.

With hindsight, Sloboda's enthusiasm might be viewed somewhat differently, and as more directly a product of the specific intellectual moment than was the impression at the time. Lerdahl and Jackendoff's theory (and some others too) certainly did generate a stream of empirical work but arguably did not establish the 'paradigmatic science' that Sloboda anticipated. Nonetheless, after a period in the 1960s and 1970s when the small amount of active research in music psychology was largely focused on highly abstracted and rather un-music-like materials

---

[6] The review, which makes very interesting reading as a survey of the psychology of music at that time by one of its leading figures, can be found in Sloboda (1992).

[7] 'Cognition and real music: the psychology of music comes of age', was first published in the journal *Psychologica Belgica* in 1986 but is more easily obtained as Chapter 5 within the collection of John Sloboda's writings entitled *Exploring the Musical Mind* (Sloboda, 2005).

(isolated pitches and durations), Lerdahl and Jackendoff's theory coincided with, and stimulated, an engagement with more musically realistic materials. This was important in making links between music psychology, and musicology and music theory, and in the UK saw the start of a much wider acceptance of music psychology by musical academia than had ever been the case before. Prior to the mid 1980s, there had been little contact (or mutual respect) between these communities, but by the early 1990s, British university music departments were appointing staff with a specific expertise in music psychology and starting to offer undergraduate and postgraduate programmes that contained, or even specialized in, music psychology.

Perhaps driven by this cultural change (the emergence of music psychology from psychology departments, and into music departments), a further transformation of the field began to take place, the consequences of which are still very evident. The structuralist-cognitive phase of music psychology – typified by Lerdahl and Jackendoff's theory and Carol Krumhansl's influential empirical work – had been consistent both with prevailing trends in Anglo-American music theory and musicology (for example a concern with formalist analysis and structuralism more generally) and with Anglo-American cognitive psychology and the new hybrid 'cognitive science', which combined psychology with artificial intelligence and computer science. A reaction against what was perceived as the quantitative and formalist character of these traditions began to take shape in the early 1990s, and music psychology – without abandoning the cognitive tradition that it had embraced so effectively – started to branch out in more qualitative, social, and developmental directions.[8] An example of this is Jeanne Bamberger's 1991 book entitled *The Mind behind the Musical Ear*, which adopted a highly focused approach to the detailed study of a small number of children in order to discover something about the specific character of children's musical minds. The approach was

---

[8] There is a strong parallel here with the debates that took place around the emergence of New Musicology, and New Paradigm research in psychology – both of which were concerned with a turn against formalism and 'quantitativism', and an enthusiasm for a more contextually sensitive, phenomenological, and hermeneutic approach to their fields.

directly influenced by the methods used by the Swiss developmental psychologist Jean Piaget, and made use of far more qualitative and individually tailored materials and investigations than would typically be true for most research using cognitive psychological methods with adults. A practical reason for this is that children (particularly young children and infants) simply will not respond to, or put up with, many standard empirical research methods: it is clearly ludicrous to ask a six month old (and probably a six year old too) to rate a melody on a numerical scale, or to indicate whether two melodies are the same or different. As has already been discussed in Chapter 8, ingenious methods *have* been devised to assess whether very young infants can discriminate between musical materials (see also section 10.4), but the developmental psychological research of the 1980s and 1990s (for instance, looking at children's songs or invented notations) often started out with a qualitative and descriptive approach, simply recording (in the broad sense of that term) what it was that children did musically in relatively naturalistic situations.

In a similar way, research on performance (which had seen a dramatic increase in activity in the later 1980s, influenced by the availability of new computer technology) started to show signs of an impatience with the generative, structuralist, and individualist approach, and began to branch out into a more social domain concerned with communication both between performers and between performers and their audiences. This made a connection with research in musical emotion and meaning – and various kinds of qualitative or more mixed (qualitative and quantitative) methods began to develop. Rather than just looking at the computer-based records of what performers produced, researchers began to pay attention to what they *said* about their own performances – a source of evidence that it might seem strange to have overlooked in the first place![9] An important precedent had been set here by researchers in ethnomusicology, who for decades had been arguing for the importance of paying very close attention to the observable behaviours of musicians in their

---

[9] A striking example of this is the book-length investigation of performance by Roger Chaffin et al. (2002), which resulted from a collaboration between a professional pianist (Imreh), a cognitive psychologist (Chaffin), and a social psychologist (Crawford).

own cultures, including what they said and wrote about their own music.[10] The ethnomusicological technique of participant observation (observing and describing a musical culture from the 'inside') shows how revealing it can be to try to understand 'musicking'[11] through close interaction with indigenous musicians – and in particular, to listen to and watch carefully what they play, say, and do. The sociologist Tia DeNora has also been influential in this regard, her book *Music in Everyday Life*, published in 2000, documenting some of the many ways in which people encounter and use music in their daily lives, largely through interviews, diaries, and covert or participant observation. For example, in looking at the ways in which music affects people's behaviour in shops, DeNora and a research associate observed the ways in which other people behaved in shops in relation to the music being played (covert observation), and on other occasions equipped themselves with recording devices and then went shopping, speaking their own experiences and their impressions of the behaviours of others, as they occurred.

If changing intellectual currents have given rise to a more diverse range of empirical methods and conceptual frameworks, then changes in technology have also had a profound impact on how music psychology has developed. The development of electronic laboratory equipment in the 1960s facilitated developments in psychoacoustics and early cognitive psychology of music, but it was the arrival and subsequent development of the desktop computer from about 1980, with associated developments in sound synthesis and MIDI technology,[12] that really underpinned the rapid development and diversification of music cognition research. Similarly, in the period since about the mid-1990s,[13]

---

10 See, among many other examples, the work by Bruno Nettl (1983), Alan Merriam (1964), or Mantle Hood (1971).

11 The term 'musicking' is the creation of Christopher Small, whose 1998 book argues that music should be understood as an act and not a thing, and that the act includes all kinds of activities (such as putting up the posters for a concert) that are typically excluded from the definitions of 'music'.

12 MIDI stands for musical instrument digital interface – a specific communication protocol for connecting keyboards, synthesizers, and computers.

13 1990–2000 was declared the 'Decade of the Brain' by President George Bush as a Library of Congress/National Institute of Mental Health initiative, causing increased funding to be made available for neuroscientific research.

developments in the technology and techniques of neuroscience – particularly the technology of brain scanning – have given rise to dramatic progress in neuroscientific investigations of musicking (listening, performing, improvising, imagining, remembering). The previously very crude neuroscientific understanding of music (such as 'music is in the right side of the brain') has been replaced by a much more fascinating and complex view of the neurological basis of a whole range of human musical functions, in both normal and clinical contexts.

10.2 **How the discipline looks now**

How, then, does music psychology look towards the end of the first decade of the twenty-first century? A simple 'measure' of the dominating preoccupations of the discipline can be derived from the distribution of topics in the proposals submitted to the recent large-scale international music psychology meeting, which took place in Sapporo, Japan, in the summer of 2008. Every two years, there is an International Conference on Music Perception and Cognition (ICMPC), bringing together a number of international societies involved in the psychology of music. The first ICMPC took place over three days in Kyoto, Japan, in 1989, with a little under a hundred papers presented. In 2008, the conference returned to Japan, following meetings in Europe, Australia, Korea, and the United States in the intervening years, and took place over a period of five days, during which papers and posters were presented in a number of parallel sessions – from an initial submission of nearly 500 proposals.

In order to facilitate organizing papers into themed sessions and symposia, the organizers of ICMPC10 asked each submitting author to indicate up to three topic areas that would best represent the proposal. The upper part of Table 10.1 shows the frequency with which each of the 22 available topics was selected by the submitting authors, and the lower part lists the six broad categories into which these 22 topics can be clustered. A number of simple observations can be made from the figures in the table. First, as the lower panel demonstrates, a broadly cognitive approach still dominates, with nearly half of all the submissions being within the first two categories (perception and cognition, and performance). From the more detailed picture presented in the

Table 10.1 Numbers (and, for the broad categories, percentages) of topics indicated in submissions to ICMPC10 (Sapporo, Japan, 2008), organized according to 22 themes and six broad categories

Theme	No.
1. Pitch, scale, and melody	45
2. Harmony and tonality	41
3. Rhythm, metre, and timing	75
4. Timbre and orchestration	16
5. Aesthetic perception and response	67
6. Emotion in music	91
7. Memory and music	38
8. Improvisation, composition, and performance	75
9. Sight-reading and memorization	5
10. Music acoustics and psychophysics	45
11. Music and neuroscience	72
12. Music education	82
13. Musical development	55
14. Music, meaning, and language	58
15. Social psychology of music	78
16. Ecological psychology of music	30
17. Cognitive musicology	48
18. Music therapy	25
19. Ethnomusicology	10
20. Computational models	62
21. Cross-cultural approach	25
22. Pedagogy and promotion of music psychology	6
Broad category (using the preceding themes)	**No. (%)**
Perception and cognition (1, 2, 3, 4, 7, 10, 17, 20)	370 (35%)
Performance (8, 9)	80 (8%)
Emotion/meaning/social (5, 6, 14, 15)	294 (28%)
Education/development/therapy (12, 13, 18)	162 (16%)
Ethno/ecology (16, 19, 21)	65 (6%)
Neuroscience (11)	72 (7%)

upper part, it is interesting to see that within this broad cognitive category there are as many papers on rhythm and timbre as there are on pitch – a very different picture from the first ICMPC, where research on pitch was overwhelmingly prevalent. Because the frequency processing characteristics of the ear are an obvious and fascinating aspect of its anatomy and physiology, and because of the enormous emphasis on pitch in music theory, music psychology was for a long time also dominated by studies of pitch. More recently, however, rhythm and timing have attracted increasing research attention, partly as a reaction against the domination of pitch and partly because of the way in which rhythm in its broadest sense is crucially involved in musical performance and communication. Second, an educational perspective, which was almost entirely absent from earlier ICMPC meetings, has gained considerable momentum, together with the emotion/meaning/social category. The significant presence of submissions in music education and the social psychology of music for ICMPC10 indicates increasing interest in more applied aspects of music psychology – and perhaps recognition of the limitations of laboratory-style research on what has often been presented as the fundamentals of music (the perception and cognition of 'primary' musical materials – pitches, rhythms, melody). The 'primary materials' outlook is based on a specific view of music (as an object, abstracted from its contexts, uses, and circumstances) that was increasingly challenged within musicology in the last decade of the twentieth century, and the prospect of an all-conquering 'cognitive science of music', powered by the methods and principles of the physical and computational sciences, has started to look very much less plausible than it once did to some people. And finally, despite its high profile, work in the neurosciences of music still represents a relatively very small proportion of the research.

Before attributing too much significance, however, to these broad features of the figures in the table, a couple of words of caution. The ICMPC website explicitly states that the founding of the ICMPC came out of the 'cognitive revolution' of the late 1950s and 1960s, and that despite the growth and diversification of the field, research in music perception and cognition remains 'central to every conference'. The organizing committee for each ICMPC does not necessarily align itself entirely with these statements and principles, but it is perhaps not too surprising to find that perception and cognition dominate the programme. Other disciplines, which overlap with the psychology of music, have their own large conferences, and this is one obvious reason why certain approaches are less well represented than might have been expected. Music therapy, for instance, has had its own World Congress of Music Therapy series since 1974; and three major conferences in New York, Venice, and Leipzig (2000, 2002, and 2005, respectively) focused specifically on evolutionary and neuroscientific perspectives on music. Music education, ethnomusicology, popular music, systematic and interdisciplinary musicology, and music theory all have their own very active international conference series, and to varying degrees, research that includes a broadly psychological component can be found in all of these. In one sense, this is an indication of the way in which music psychology has been increasingly widely accepted, and incorporated into the broader study of music – but this assimilation can also have the effect of making the 'core' of the subject appear more doggedly cognitive than is actually the case.

The distribution of research topics represented in Table 10.1 is strikingly different from the picture presented at the equivalent conference just 12 years earlier (ICMPC4, McGill, Canada, 1996): the proceedings from that conference contain not a single paper on music education, music therapy, or music in everyday life, and over 30% of the papers in the volume are concerned with pitch. An overwhelming 80% of the papers fall into the 'perception and cognition' category. Twelve years on, alongside the continuing interest in a cognitive approach, there are now the perspectives offered by biological and cultural evolution;[14] social psychology and the functions of music in everyday life; a resurgence of interest in emotion, meaning, and communication in music; and an awareness of the importance of the body in music – ranging from the 'macro' level of bodily gesture and movement in the production and perception of music, to the 'micro' level of neuroscientific studies of music and the brain.

---

[14] For example, see the work by Colwyn Trevarthen (1999–2000), Nils Wallin et al. (2000), Elizabeth Tolbert (2001), and Ian Cross (2003).

10.3 **Preoccupations and blind spots**

As music psychology has changed and developed in a number of different ways over the century or more of its existence as a recognized subject, it has inevitably been preoccupied with, or conversely blind to, different questions at different times. If we confine ourselves to the development of the 'modern' psychology of music – from about 1980 onwards – then the overriding preoccupation of the cognitive psychology of music (up to the mid 1990s) was the question of musical structure: how listeners formed mental representations of musical structures as they heard or remembered music, and how performers made use of, or responded to, musical structures as they played music expressively or tried to read and memorize it. Tonal and rhythmic structures have loomed extremely large in this landscape, and other aspects of musical structure and sound (such as timbre, dynamics, texture, and spatialization) have received less attention. The 'cultural positioning' of music psychology (its domination by Anglo-American researchers) has meant that classical Western tonal music has been the overwhelming focus of attention, and investigations of the music of other cultures have usually been somewhat superficial – and virtually always motivated by the desire to do the kind of cross-cultural comparison of which ethnomusicologists are often understandably suspicious. It is all too easy for a comparison of Western listener behaviour with, for example, Javanese listeners to start off with deeply rooted ethnocentric assumptions (about the nature and function of listening, for instance), which then ensure that a similarly ethnocentrically-specific 'result' will be found. The same broad problem often applies to investigations of the music of subcultures that are geographically much closer to home (pop and jazz) but which may also involve radically different basic assumptions and kinds of behaviour.

The concentration on cognition meant that for a long time emotion and meaning in music remained virtually an untouched subject. The argument for this was that people's emotional responses to music, and what music might mean to them, were so unpredictable and idiosyncratic, and so dependent on personality or biographical and contextual factors, that it was simply impossible to make progress in that direction in any systematic or empirically defensible fashion. Because structure was regarded as the bedrock in relation to which musical experience should be understood, the first step must be to understand how people pick up and represent structure – after which the mystery of emotion and meaning could be tackled. Only more recently has the research community become impatient with this attitude – not only because the 'holy grail' never seemed to get any nearer but also because the commitment to a structuralist approach to practically all musical issues began to be seriously questioned on more fundamental grounds – as described in Section 10.1. Research on emotion in music, in relation to both listening and performing, has now become a much more active area, as have the related themes of embodiment, gesture, meaning, and the functions of music in everyday life.

The use of mixed qualitative and quantitative methods has brought about a convergence between music psychology, ethnomusicology, and the sociology of music, but with significantly different agendas and conceptual frameworks, allowing substantially different questions to be addressed.[15] Take, for example, the case of jazz musicians playing together. From a broadly sociological/ethnomusicological perspective, the primary focus of interest here might be the ways in which those musicians talk about their experiences, how they construct their own sense of identity and musical value within that context, detailed descriptions of the kinds of interactions that can be observed between them in performance, and perhaps an analysis of the power and authority structures that control those interactions.[16] By contrast, music psychologists have been more concerned with trying to understand how it is that performing musicians in this kind of improvising context can control the time course and specific content of their interactions from the point of view of sensorimotor control and communicative interaction,

---

15 Nicholas Cook has discussed the wide-ranging adoption of what were previously regarded as purely ethnomusicological principles in the study of music in a chapter entitled 'We are all (ethno)musicologists now' (2008).

16 These, and other insights and analyses, are contained in Paul Berliner's *Thinking in Jazz: The Infinite Art of Improvisation* (1994) and Ingrid Monson's *Saying Something: Jazz Improvisation and Interaction* (1996).

and what they are specifically doing to produce, for instance, a sense of 'groove', or a 'laid back' feel, and how that might be affected by context and intention. There is a complementarity between these kinds of approach, and although a frustration with what is regarded as either the 'naïve empiricism' of the psychologist or the 'lack of explanatory rigour' of the ethnomusicologist may sometimes surface, the aim must surely be to try to find the connecting threads between these different views. There are signs that such an approach is starting to emerge in various relationships between music psychology, ethnomusicology, sociology of music, anthropology, archaeology, and ecology.[17]

One of the blind spots of earlier psychology of music was a rather stark de-socialization of its subject matter – a tendency to treat musical behaviour as the cognitive skills of an individual listener, performer, or composer. In part, this reflects a dominating view within older musicology and music theory in which music is seen in a distinctly abstracted and autonomous light: organized sound in time. This view of music fitted rather too neatly with the ways in which music might be investigated in a laboratory context, which for most of the twentieth century was how psychological research was generally carried out. In part, this can be attributed to the grip that a positivist empiricism, based on laboratory methods and hypothesis testing, has had on music psychology and psychology more generally – and perhaps the discipline's desire to exploit its association with the prestige (and superior funding) of the natural sciences. Because this dominant method had such a determining influence on what was regarded as the appropriate subject matter, it is important to have some sense of what the typical methods used in music psychology have been – which is the aim of the next section.

10.4 **Methods**

A discipline is characterized or defined as much by its methods as by the subject matter to which it lays claim. This is particularly true of music

---

[17] See, for example, the following articles and books: DeNora (2000, 2003), Cross (2003), Huron (2004, 2008), Clarke (2005b), Clayton et al. (2005), Miell et al. (2005), Mithen (2005), and Pitts (2005a).

psychology, because a good deal of its 'subject matter' (What do people hear? What does music mean? Why do people have emotional responses to music? How do people play music? How do children develop musical skills? Is it possible to understand people's musical preferences? Where does music come from?) is common to other disciplines – such as music theory, music education, the sociology of music, aesthetics, and human evolution. One of the things that identifies these as topics in music psychology are the particular methods used to investigate them – as well as the conceptual frameworks that are deployed.[18]

Not surprisingly, in the light of its history, music psychology has inherited many of its methods from psychology generally and experimental cognitive psychology more specifically. The cognitive revolution of the late 1950s and early 1960s was as much a revolution in laboratory methods as anything else, and many of these were imported directly into music research. Typical laboratory studies involved the presentation of controlled musical materials to individual participants (nearly always called 'subjects' in research prior to the 1990s) who were required to make perceptual judgements about them. These judgements might involve rating items on numerical scales of various kinds or indicating whether pairs of items were the same or different. For example, in a number of studies of short-term memory for melodies undertaken in the 1970s and 1980s, Jay Dowling and his various coworkers presented pairs of simple melodies, each perhaps no more than five or seven notes long and separated by a brief pause, and asked listeners to judge whether the pairs were the same or different under various conditions of transposition and alteration. Similar kinds of procedure might require listeners to judge whether a specific chord in a sequence of chords was in tune or not (the speed at which the judgement was made acting as an indicator of various kinds of cognitive processing) or, in a method developed by Carol Krumhansl and known as the

---

[18] A survey and discussion of different empirical methods in music research – including sociological, psychological, ethnomusicological, and musicological methods – can be found in Eric Clarke and Nicholas Cook's edited book *Empirical Musicology: Aims, Methods, Prospects* (2004).

'probe-tone technique', to judge how well a single note fit with various kinds of prior context.

In psychological studies of musical performance, which developed out of studies of other kinds of 'performance' such as speaking and typewriting, the methods have usually tried to capture specific aspects of what performers do in controlled but ideally reasonably realistic ways. Detailed studies of the timing, dynamics, articulation, and physical movements of skilled musical performances can be carried out in order to investigate a whole range of research questions about expression, emotion, communication, and style change. The performances are either recorded directly from musical instruments (usually keyboards) linked to computers; or from various methods of extracting similar information from commercial sound recordings – or video in the case of body movement. As with the listening studies mentioned earlier, what is gathered are numerical data – in this case large bodies of it, because even a short period of piano playing can generate thousands or tens of thousands of bits of information. All of these approaches are variants of the standard quantitative methods of experimental psychology, giving rise to the type of numerical or categorical data (reaction times, values on a five-point scale, yes/no judgements, durations and intensities) that can be analysed using standard statistical methods.

There are some significant advantages to carrying out this kind of controlled and quantitative research: the data are clearly defined, the methods are quite well established, the principles are widely known and accepted in the general scientific community, and the analytical techniques are readily available in standard computer software. Nonetheless, there are limitations: many kinds of musical behaviour are complex and continuous and cannot easily be reduced to the discrete judgements that quantitative research typically requires. If the aim is to find out something about listeners' fluctuating emotional responses to music, for example, then it can be hard to design a realistic study that produces neat, quantitative data. There have been attempts to capture more continuous quantitative data, for instance, by asking listeners to move a computer mouse around so as to convey their changing emotional response to music, but it is equally likely that a researcher will ask participants to talk freely about what they heard, or keep a written or spoken diary of their listening experiences over a significant period of time. These are qualitative data – potentially rich and complex statements that cannot be reduced to points on a scale – and they present different challenges and opportunities to the researchers who use them.

Until quite recently, qualitative research was regarded as the poor relation of its more hard-nosed quantitative counterpart, but in the 1990s there was a significant change in this attitude, and qualitative research is now much more widely accepted and correspondingly more methodologically developed.[19] There are now accepted ways to analyse qualitative data ('grounded theory' and 'interpretative phenomenological analysis' are two of them) that provide frameworks within which to analyse complex and often messy qualitative data (spoken language, diaries, open-ended interviews, video images) with a degree of system and rigour. Social and developmental psychology have always been much more ready to use a qualitative approach, often combined with quantitative methods of the kind that are typically found in questionnaires. If you are interested in finding out about teenagers' musical preferences, for example, it is likely that you will want to talk to some teenagers in an informal and open-ended way, and perhaps also send out a questionnaire to a much larger sample to get some kind of overview. The interviews will yield qualitative data (recorded conversations), and the questionnaires might either produce quantitative data, if the questions ask for ratings or multiple choice answers, or additional qualitative data if they simply ask for 'free-form' written answers to the corresponding questions.

A different example of a mixed method of this kind is the so-called Experience Sampling Method (ESM). ESM makes use of mobile phones or pagers to contact people at unanticipated times at which they then record in some way something about their musical experience. For example, in a study by John Sloboda, Susan O'Neill, and Antonia Ivaldi, students and staff at a UK university were contacted by pager

---

[19] Colin Robson's *Real World Research* (2002) gives a very accessible account of both quantitative and qualitative methods for research in 'everyday' settings. See also Smith (2003).

and asked to note at the time of contact whether they were in the presence of any music and under what circumstances.[20] The resulting information, which consisted of both qualitative and quantitative data, was used to build up a picture of the degree and nature of people's exposure to, and use of, music in their everyday lives.

Certain kinds of research necessarily require the use of rather specialized methods, and working with young infants is one such example. If you are interested in knowing whether a three-week-old infant can recognize her mother's singing, for example, you can neither ask the infant nor expect her to press one of two buttons for 'yes' or 'no'! But some ingenious methods have been devised by developmental psychologists that do allow such research to be carried out. Even very young infants have been found to turn to look at objects or events they find interesting, and have also been found to suck faster on a dummy when their interest and attention are engaged. With equipment that can monitor the direction of gaze or sucking rate, researchers have been able to investigate the music-perceptual capacities and preferences of infants that are days or even just hours old, as discussed in Chapter 8.

Finally, research into music and neuroscience (the activity of the brain when people hear, play, compose, or imagine music) requires very specialized methods. The various kinds of brain imaging techniques, such as functional magnetic resonance imaging (fMRI), positron-emission tomography (PET), magnetoencephalography (MEG), and electroencephalography (EEG), are all different ways of monitoring how much activity is going on in different areas of the brain, using electrical activity, or the amount of blood flowing to that part of the brain, or oxygen consumed, as the indicator (the more active is a part of the brain, the more oxygen, carried by the blood, does it need). All of these techniques have their own particular strengths and weaknesses, relating to their spatial and temporal resolution, and noisiness, determining the kinds of study in which they can be used. For example, some of the machines needed to monitor blood flow are extremely invasive for the participant, who may have to lie with his or her head completely engulfed by

---

[20] This study is reported in a paper by Sloboda et al. (2001).

what looks like a very large and noisy tumble dryer. The information that can be gathered about different regions of brain activity is potentially fascinating, and rapid advances have been made since the 1990s in what is known about general (as well as musically specific) brain functioning, but it is obviously very hard under these physical circumstances to involve people in anything like realistic musical activities.

The methods of music psychology, therefore, strongly reflect more general methodological and conceptual developments taking place in the wider psychological community, and in other disciplines (neuroscience, anthropology, sociology, acoustics, cultural studies) that overlap with it. There are few, if any, methods that are absolutely specific to music psychology, perhaps indicating that music psychology is more concerned with establishing an identity on the basis of the phenomena that it investigates rather than by virtue of its approaches. But how successful has music psychology been in investigating musical phenomena that have a bearing on people's actual experience of music? Has the concentration on a cognitive approach discussed earlier in this chapter allowed music psychology to shed light on the experiences and skills that people really want to know about? And has the psychology of music had any real impact on the understanding or practical activities of those people who do the 'musicking' (to use Christopher Small's term again) – listeners, players, composers, and teachers?

10.5 Practical reality and academic research

At the end of a collection of writings spanning 30 years of his research career, John Sloboda offered a challenge to the field to which he himself has made major contributions:

> A question which I have posed repeatedly to anyone who will listen is: suppose all the music psychology in the world had never been written, and was expunged from the collective memory of the world, as if it had never existed, how would music and musicians be disadvantaged? Would composers compose less good music, would performers cease to perform so well, would those who enjoy listening to it enjoy it any less richly?[21]

---

[21] See Sloboda (2005, pp. 395–396).

Implicit in these questions, and made more explicit towards the end of the chapter in which they appear, is the premise that research in the psychology of music should have practical application to the real situations of composing, performing, and listening to music. But is it appropriate to think that the psychology of music should ever have tried to address any of those practical functions – or, to put it in a different way, should they represent the primary criterion by which the success or legitimacy of the discipline is measured? An alternative is to regard the psychology of music as a way of trying to understand a particularly fascinating and exceptionally widespread aspect of human culture and human mentality – and in doing so, helping to advance the broader goal of trying to understand human beings. This aim is arguably more crucial to any claims for the 'real-world' or social relevance of music psychology than the more concrete improvements to musicking that Sloboda points to in the extract from his book. The connection may at times seem remote, but given the importance of music in many people's lives in cultures all over the world, a deeper understanding of people's musicking may be one way to achieve wider understanding of people and their social context, in all their cultural and subjective diversity. Music can be understood both as an engagement with fascinating sounds and behaviours and as a way of gaining insight into other times and other cultures – and perhaps, through music psychology, other consciousnesses and subjectivities.[22] Many of the world's 'big problems' are attributable to a failure of understanding, and if research in music can help us all to arrive at a better understanding of one another, then there might be nothing wrong with the 'no' answers that are rhetorically implied by John Sloboda's questions.

This might appear an unrealistically idealistic response to his challenge – and one that could even be accused of retreating behind such a 'cerebral' view that it simply avoids the question. A different response to the challenge of music psychology's practical relevance is to point to the increasing enthusiasm of researchers to engage with music in its real-world settings: in education and therapy, in shops and

---

[22] See Cook (1998, p. 129) and Clarke (2005b, p. 90).

advertising, in orchestras and at pop gigs, in the context of religious worship, and in performers' practice and recording studios. Whether this will have an impact on the excellence of performers', composers', and listeners' skills and achievements is another matter; but that may be something that should be left to educators, composers, and teachers or players themselves. Perhaps it is both unrealistic and presumptuous to assume that researchers will (or even should) have anything practical to offer to activities that have developed in complex cultural contexts over the entire course of human history. There may be some areas in which systematic research can help to overcome specific impediments to progress, but in general those who are directly involved with music have a direct 'feel' for what they are doing and how to make progress – however narrowly focused, intuitive, and at times poorly expressed that understanding may seem. Systematic research inevitably tends to be less directly in touch with the stuff itself and more dispassionate and distanced – which is part of what defines it as research. We should be happy with this productive complementarity rather than trying always to achieve some kind of comforting synthesis.

References

Ansdell, G. (1995) *Music for Life: Aspects of Creative Music Therapy with Adult Clients.* London: Jessica Kingsley.

Baddeley, A. (1997) *Human Memory: Theory and Practice.* Hove: Psychology Press.

Bailey, B.A. & Davidson, J.W. (2002) Adaptive characteristics of group singing: perceptions from members of a choir for homeless men. *Musicae Scientiae,* 6(2): 221–256.

Bailey, D. (1992) *Improvisation. Its Nature and Practice in Music.* London: The British Library.

Baily, J. (1985) Music structure and human movement. In P. Howell, I. Cross, & R. West (Eds.) *Musical Structure and Cognition.* New York: Academic Press, 237–258.

Baker, D. (2005) Peripatetic music teachers approaching mid-career: a cause for concern? *British Journal of Music Education,* 22(2): 141–154.

Balkwill, L-L. & Thompson, W.F. (1999) A cross-cultural investigation of the perception of emotion in music: psychophysical cues and cultural cues. *Music Perception,* 17(1): 43–64.

Bamberger, J.S. (1991) *The Mind Behind the Musical Ear: How Children Develop Musical Intelligence.* Cambridge, MA: Harvard University Press.

Barker, A. (Ed.) (1989) *Greek Musical Writings.* Cambridge: Cambridge University Press.

Barrett, H.C. & Kurzban, R. (2006) Modularity in cognition: framing the debate. *Psychological Review,* 113: 628–647.

BBC News (2003) Sesame Street breaks Iraqi POWs (updated 20 May). Available at: http://news/bbc.co.uk/l/hi/world/middle_east/3042907.stm (accessed 28 July 2009).

BBC News (2004a) Drivers warned against loud music (updated 14 April). Available at: http://news.bbc.co.uk/1/hi/uk/3623237.stm (accessed 11 May 2005).

BBC News (2004b) Shops go classical to combat yobs (updated 18 August). Available at: http://news.bbc.co.uk/1/hi/uk/3576878.stm (accessed 11 May 2005).

BBC News (2004c) Classics deter bus station yobs (updated 23 August). Available at: http://news.bbc.co.uk/1/hi/england/humber/3592320.stm (accessed 11 May 2005).

BBC News (2005a) Vandals driven away by loud tunes (updated 8 March). Available at: http://news.bbc.co.uk/1/hi/england/hereford/worcs/4329739.stm (accessed 11 May 2005).

BBC News (2005b) Classical solution to anti-social behaviour (updated 11 May). Available at: http://news.bbc.co.uk/1/hi/northern_ireland/4534537.stm (accessed 11 May 2005).

Becker, J. (2004) *Deep Listeners: Music, Emotion and Trancing*. Bloomington, IN: Indiana University Press.

Berliner, P. (1994) *Thinking in Jazz: The Infinite Art of Improvisation*. Chicago, IL: University of Chicago Press.

Berlyne, D.E. (1971) *Aesthetics and Psychobiology*. New York: Appleton-Century-Crofts.

Born, G. (2005) On musical mediation: ontology, technology and creativity. *Twentieth-Century Music*, 2: 7–36.

Borthwick, S.J. & Davidson, J.W. (2002) Developing a child's identity as a musician: a family 'script' perspective. In R. MacDonald, D.J. Hargreaves & D. Miell (Eds.) *Musical Identities*. Oxford: Oxford University Press, 60–78.

Bourdieu, P. (1984) *Distinction: A Social Critique of the Judgement of Taste*. London: Routledge.

Bregman, A.S. (1990) *Auditory Scene Analysis. The Perceptual Organization of Sound*. Cambridge, MA: MIT Press.

Brodsky, W. (2002) The effects of music tempo on simulated driving performance and vehicular control. *Transportation Research Part F*, 4: 219–241.

Bull, M. (2000) *Sounding Out the City: Personal Stereos and the Management of Everyday Life*. Oxford: Berg.

Bull, M. (2007) *Sound Moves: iPod Culture and Urban Experience*. London: Routledge.

Bunt, L. (1994) *Music Therapy: An Art beyond Words*. London: Routledge.

Campbell, P.S. (1998) *Songs in Their Heads: Music and Its Meaning in Children's Lives*. Oxford: Oxford University Press.

Chaffin, R., Imreh, G. & Crawford, M. (2002) *Practicing Perfection. Memory and Piano Performance*. Mahwah, NJ: Lawrence Erlbaum.

Chase, W.G. & Simon, H.A. (1973) The mind's eye in chess. In W.G. Chase (Ed.) *Visual Information Processing*. New York: Academic Press, 215–281.

Clarke, E.F. (1988) Generative principles in music performance. In J.A. Sloboda (Ed.) *Generative Processes in Music*. Oxford: Clarendon Press, 1–26.

Clarke, E.F. (2002) Understanding the psychology of performance. In J. Rink (Ed.) *Musical Performance. A Guide to Understanding*. Cambridge: Cambridge University Press, 59–72.

Clarke, E.F. (2005a) Creativity in performance. *Musicae Scientiae*, 9: 157–182.

Clarke, E.F. (2005b) *Ways of Listening: An Ecological Approach to the Perception of Musical Meaning*. New York: Oxford University Press.

Clarke, E.F. & Cook, N. (Eds.) (2004) *Empirical Musicology: Aims, Methods, Prospects*. Oxford: Oxford University Press.

Clarke, E.F. & Davidson, J.W. (1998) The body in music. In W. Thomas (Ed.) *Composition-Performance-Reception. Studies in the Creative Process in Music*. Aldershot: Ashgate Press, 74–92.

Clayton, M., Sager, R. & Will, U. (2005) In time with the music: the concept of entrainment and its significance for ethnomusicology. *European Meetings in Ethnomusicology*, 11(ESEM Counterpoint 1): 3–75.

Clynes, M. (Ed.) (1982) *Music, Mind and Brain: The Neuropsychology of Music*. New York: Plenum Press.

Coffman, D. (2002) Banding together: new horizons in lifelong music making. *Journal of Aging and Identity*, 7: 133–143.

Collins, D. (2005) A synthesis process model of creative thinking in music composition. *Psychology of Music*, 33: 193–216.

Cook, N. (1994) Perception: a perspective from music theory. In R. Aiello & J.A. Sloboda (Eds.) *Musical Perceptions*. New York: Oxford University Press, 64–95.

Cook, N. (1998) *Music: A Very Short Introduction*. Oxford: Oxford University Press.

Cook, N. (2001) Theorizing musical meaning. *Music Theory Spectrum*, 23: 170–195.

Cook, N. (2004) Making music together, or improvisation and its others. *The Source: Challenging Jazz Criticism*, 1: 5–25. Also reprinted in Cook, N. (2007) *Music, Performance, Meaning: Selected Essays*. Aldershot: Ashgate Press.

Cook, N. (2008) We are all (ethno)musicologists now. In H. Stobart (Ed.) *The New (Ethno)musicologies*. Lanham, MD: Scarecrow Press, 48–70.

Cooke, D. (1959) *The Language of Music*. Oxford: Oxford University Press.

Cope, P. (2005) Adult learning in traditional music. *British Journal of Music Education*, 22: 125–140.

Costa-Giomi, E. (1999) The effects of three years of piano instruction on children's cognitive development. *Journal of Research in Music Education*, 47(5): 198–22.

Cox, G.S.A. (1999) Secondary school music teachers talking. *Music Education Research*, 1: 37–46.

Cross, I. (1998) Music analysis and music perception. *Music Analysis*, 17: 3–20.

Cross, I. (1999) Is music the most important thing we ever did? Music, development and evolution. In S.W.Yi (Ed.) *Music, Mind and Science*, Seoul: Seoul National University Press.

Cross, I. (2003) Music and biocultural evolution. In M. Clayton, T. Herbert & R. Middleton (Eds.) *The Cultural Study of Music. A Critical Introduction*. London: Routledge, 19–30.

Cross. I. (2009) The nature of music and its evolution. In S. Hallam, I. Cross & M. Thaut (Eds.) *The Oxford Handbook of Music Psychology*. Oxford: Oxford University Press, 3–13.

Crowder, R. (1993) Auditory memory. In S. McAdams & E. Bigand (Eds.) *Thinking in Sound: The Cognitive Psychology of Human Audition*. Oxford: Oxford University Press, 113–145.

Csikszentmihályi, M. (1975) *Beyond Boredom and Anxiety*. San Francisco, CA: Jossey-Bass.

Csikszentmihályi, M. (1990) *Flow: The Psychology of Optimal Experience*. New York: Harper & Row.

Cusick, S. (2008) 'You are in a place that is out of the world…': music in the detention camps of the 'Global War on Terror'. *Journal of the Society for American Music*, 2: 1–26.

Davidson, J.W. (2001) The role of the body in the production and perception of solo vocal performance: a case study of Annie Lennox. *Musicae Scientiae*, 5: 235–256.

Davidson, J.W. (2002) Communicating with the body in performance. In J. Rink (Ed.) *Musical Performance. A Guide to Understanding*. Cambridge: Cambridge University Press, 144–152.

Davidson, J.W. & Burland, K. (2006) Musician identity formation. In G.E. McPherson (Ed.) *The Child as Musician: A Handbook of Musical Development*. Oxford: Oxford University Press, 475–490.

Davidson, J.W. & Correia, J.S. (2002) Body movement. In R. Parncutt & G. McPherson (Eds.) *The Science and Psychology of Music Performance: Creative Strategies for Teaching and Learning*. New York: Oxford University Press, 237–251.

Davies, C. (1986) Say it till a song comes: reflections on songs invented by children 3–13. *British Journal of Music Education*, 3: 279–293.

Davies, C. (1992) Listen to my song: a study of songs invented by children aged 5 to 7 years. *British Journal of Music Education*, 9: 19–48.

Davies, J.B. (1978) *The Psychology of Music*. London: Hutchinson.

Deliège, I. & Sloboda, J.A. (Eds.) (1996) *Musical Beginnings: Origins and Development of Musical Competence*. Oxford: Oxford University Press.

DeNora, T. (2000) *Music in Everyday Life*. Cambridge: Cambridge University Press.

DeNora, T. (2003) *After Adorno. Rethinking Music Sociology*. Cambridge: Cambridge University Press.

Deutsch, D., Gabrielsson, A., Sloboda, J., Cross, I., Drake, C., Parncutt, R., et al. Psychology of Music. In *Grove Music Online*. Oxford Music Online. Available at: http://www.oxfordmusiconline.com/subscriber/article/grove/music/42574 (accessed 28 July 2009).

Deutsch, D. (Ed.) (1982) *The Psychology of Music*. New York: Academic Press.

Dibben, N. (2001) What do we hear when we hear music? Music perception and musical material. *Musicae Scientiae*, 5(2): 161–194.

Dibben, N. (2004) The role of peripheral feedback in emotional experience with music. *Music Perception*, 22(1): 79–116.

Dibben, N. & Williamson, V. (2007) An exploratory survey of in–vehicle music listening. *Psychology of Music*, 35(4): 571–589.

Dowling, W.J. & Harwood, D.L. (1985) *Music Cognition*. Orlando, FL: Academic Press.

Drummond, B. (2001) The classroom music teacher – inspirations, aspirations and realities. The evidence from Northern Ireland. *British Journal of Music Education*, 18: 5–26.

Eagle, C. (1996) An introductory perspective on music psychology. In D. Hodges (Ed.), *Handbook of Music Psychology*, 2nd ed. San Antonio: IMR Press, 1–28.

Ericsson, K.A., Krampe, R.T. & Tesch-Römer, C. (1993) The role of deliberate practice in the acquisition of expert performance. *Psychological Review*, 100: 363–406.

Eysenck, M.W. & Keane, M.T. (2005) *Cognitive Psychology: A Student's Handbook* (5th edition). Hove: Psychology Press.

Falk, D. (2004) Prelinguistic evolution in early hominins: Whence motherese? *Behavioral and Brain Sciences*, 27: 491–503.

Fassbender, C. (1996) Infants' auditory sensitivity towards acoustic parameter of speech and music. In I. Deliège & J. Sloboda (Eds.) *Musical Beginnings. Origins and Development of Musical Competence*. Oxford: Oxford University Press, 56–87.

Fitch, F.J. & Heyde, N. (2007) 'Recercar' – the collaborative process as invention. *Twentieth-Century Music*, 4: 71–95.

Flohr, J. & Hodges, D. (2006) Music and neuroscience. In R. Colwell (Ed.) *MENC Handbook of Musical Cognition and Development*. New York: Oxford University Press, 7–39.

Fodor, J.A. (1983) *The Modularity of Mind*. Cambridge, MA: MIT Press.

Frith, S. (2003) Music and everyday life. In M. Clayton, T. Herbert & R. Middleton (Eds.) *The Cultural Study of Music: A Critical Introduction*. London: Routledge, 92–101.

Gabrielsson, A. (1999) Music performance. In D. Deutsch (Ed.) *The Psychology of Music* (2nd edition). New York: Academic Press, 501–602.

Gabrielsson, A. (2001) Emotions in strong experiences with music. In P.N. Juslin & J.A. Sloboda (Eds.) *Music and Emotion: Theory and Research*. Oxford: Oxford University Press, 431–452.

Gaines, J. (2005) *Evening in the Palace of Reason. Bach Meets Frederick The Great in the Age of Enlightenment* London: Fourth Estate.

Gibson, J.J. (1966) *The Senses Considered as Perceptual Systems*. Boston, MA: Houghton Mifflin.

Gembris, H. (2006) The development of musical abilities. In R. Colwell (Ed.) *MENC Handbook of Musical Cognition and Development*. Oxford: Oxford University Press, 124–164.

Gembris, H. (Ed.) (2006) *Musical Development from a Lifespan Perspective*. Frankfurt: Peter Lang.

Ginsborg, J. (2004) Strategies for memorizing music. In A. Williamon (Ed.) *Musical Excellence. Strategies and Techniques to Enhance Performance*. Oxford: Oxford University Press, 123–141.

Gjerdingen, R.O. (1999) Apparent motion in music? In N. Griffith & P. Todd (Eds.) *Musical Networks. Parallel Distributed Perception and Performance*. Cambridge, MA: MIT Press, 141–173.

Goehr, L. (1992) *The Imaginary Museum of Musical Works: An Essay in the Philosophy of Music*. Oxford: Clarendon.

Green, L. (1997) *Music, Gender, Education*. Cambridge: Cambridge University Press.

Green, L. (2001) *How Popular Musicians Learn: A Way Ahead for Music Education*. Aldershot: Ashgate Press.

Gregory, A. (1997) The roles of music in society: the ethnomusicological perspective. In D.J. Hargreaves & A.C. North (Eds.) *The Social Psychology of Music*. Oxford: Oxford University Press.

Hargreaves, D.J. (1986) *The Developmental Psychology of Music*. Oxford: Oxford University Press.

Harland, J., Kinder, K., Lord, P., Stott, A., Schagen, I., Haynes, J. et al. (2000) *Arts Education in Secondary Schools: Effects and Effectiveness*. Slough: National Foundation for Educational Research.

Hays, T. & Minichiello, V. (2005) The meaning of music in the lives of older people: a qualitative study. *Psychology of Music*, 33: 437–51.

Hesse, H. (1960) *The Glassbead Game* (translated by R. Winston & C. Winston). Harmondsworth: Penguin.

Hetland, L. (2000) Listening to music enhances spatial-temporal reasoning: evidence for the 'Mozart Effect'. *Journal of Aesthetic Education*, 34(3/4): 105–148.

Hodges, D. (Ed.) (1980) *Handbook of Music Psychology*. Dubuque, IA: Kendall-Hunt.

Hodges, D. (2006) The musical brain. In G.E. McPherson (Ed.) *The Child as Musician: A Handbook of Musical Development*. Oxford: Oxford University Press, 51–68.

Hood, M. (1971) *The Ethnomusicologist*. New York: McGraw-Hill.

Hornby, N. (1995) *High Fidelity*. London: Penguin.

Hornby, N. (2003) *31 Songs*. London: Penguin.

Howell, P., Cross, I. & West, R. (Eds.) (1985) *Musical Structure and Cognition*. New York: Academic Press.

Hume, L., Dodd, C.A. & Grigg, N.P. (2003) In-store selection of wine – no evidence for the mediation of music? *Perceptual and Motor Skills*, 96(3): 1252–1254.

Huron, D. (2001) Tone and voice: a derivation of the rules of voice-leading from perceptual principles. *Music Perception*, 19: 1–64.

Huron, D. (2003) Is music an evolutionary adaptation? In I. Peretz & R. Zatorre (Eds.) *The Cognitive Neuroscience of Music*. Oxford: Oxford University Press, 57–75.

Huron, D. (2004) Issues and prospects in studying cognitive cultural diversity. In S. Lipscomb, R. Ashley, R. Gjerdingen & P. Webster (Eds.), *Proceedings of the 8th International Conference on Music Perception and Cognition*. Evanston, IL: The Society for Music Perception and Cognition, 93–95.

Huron, D. (2006) *Sweet Anticipation: Music and the Psychology of Expectation*. Cambridge, MA: MIT Press.

Huron, D. (2008) Science and music: lost in music. *Nature*, 453: 456–457.

Huron, D. & Veltman, J. (2006) A cognitive approach to medieval mode: evidence for an historical antecedent to the major/minor system. *Empirical Musicology Review*, 1(1), 33–55. Available at: http://emusicology.org/v1n1/contents2.html (accessed 12 May 2008).

Husain, G., Thompson, W.F. & Schellenberg, E.G. (2002) Effects of musical tempo and mode on arousal, mood, and spatial abilities. *Music Perception*, 20(2), 151–171.

Ivaldi, A. & O'Neill, S.A. (2008) Adolescents' musical role models: whom do they admire and why? *Psychology of Music*, 36: 395–415.

Johansson, B. (2002) Music, age, performance, and excellence: a neuroscientific approach. *Psychomusicology*, 18: 46–58.

Johnson, J. (2002) *Who Needs Classical Music?* Oxford: Oxford University Press.

Johnson, M.L. & Larson, S. (2003) 'Something in the way she moves' – metaphors of musical motion. *Metaphor and Symbol*, 18: 63–84.

Jusczyk, P.W. (1997) *The Discovery of Spoken Language*. Cambridge, MA: MIT Press.

Juslin, P.N. (2003) Five facets of musical expression: a psychologist's perspective on musical expression. *Psychology of Music*, 31: 273–302.

Juslin, P.N. (2009) Emotional responses to music. In S. Hallam, I. Cross & M. Thaut (Eds.) *The Oxford Handbook of Music Psychology*. Oxford: Oxford University Press, 131–140.

Juslin, P.N., Friberg, A. & Bresin, R. (2001–2002) Toward a computational model of expression in music performance: the GERM model. *Musicae Scientiae*, Special Issue on Current Trends in the Study of Music and Emotion, 63–122.

Kemp, A. (1996) *The Musical Temperament: Psychology and Personality of Musicians*. Oxford: Oxford University Press.

Krampe, R.T. (2006) Musical expertise from a lifespan perspective. In H. Gembris (Ed.) *Musical Development from a Lifespan Perspective*. Frankfurt: Peter Lang, 91–105.

Knobloch, S. & Zillman, D. (2002) Mood management via the Digital Jukebox. *Journal of Communication*, 52(2): 351–366.

Kronman, U. & Sundberg, J. (1987) Is the musical ritard an allusion to physical motion? In A. Gabrielsson (Ed.) *Action and Perception in Rhythm and Music*. Stockholm: Royal Swedish Academy of Music, 57–68.

Krumhansl, C.L. (1990) *Cognitive Foundations of Musical Pitch*. New York: Oxford University Press.

Krumhansl, C., Sandell, G.J. & Sergeant, D.C. (1987) Tone hierarchies and mirror forms in serial music. *Music Perception*, 5: 31–96.

Lafuente, M.J., Grifol, R., Segarra, J., Soriano, M., Gorba, A. & Montesinos, A. (1997) Effects of the Firstart method of prenatal simulation on psychomotor development: the first six months. *Pre and Perinatal Journal*, 11(3): 151–162.

Lamont, A., Hargreaves, D.J., Marshall, N.A. & Tarrant, M. (2003) Young people's music in and out of school. *British Journal of Music Education*, 20: 229–241.

Langer, S. (1951) *Philosophy in a New Key: A Study in the Symbolism of Reason, Rite and Art*. London: Oxford University Press.

Lanza, J. (2004) *Elevator Music: A Surreal History of Muzak, Easy-listening, and Other Moodsong* (2nd edition). Ann Arbor, MI: University of Michigan Press.

Large, E.W. & Jones, M.R. (1999) The dynamics of attending: how we track time-varying events. *Psychological Review*, 106: 119–159.

Lehmann, A. & McArthur, V. (2002) Sight reading. In R. Parncutt & G. McPherson (Eds.) *The Science and Psychology of Music Performance: Creative Strategies for Teaching and Learning*. New York: Oxford University Press, 135–150.

Lehmann, A., Sloboda, J.A. & Woody, R. (2007) *Psychology for Musicians*. Oxford: Oxford University Press.

Lerdahl, F. (1988) Cognitive constraints on compositional systems. In J. Sloboda (Ed.) *Generative Processes in Music. The Psychology of Performance, Improvisation, and Composition.* Oxford: Clarendon Press, 231–259.

Lerdahl, F. & Jackendoff, R. (1983) *A Generative Theory of Tonal Music.* Cambridge, MA: MIT. Press.

Lesiuk, T. (2005) The effect of music listening on work performance. *Psychology of Music*, 33(2): 173–191.

London, J. (2004) *Hearing in Time: Psychological Aspects of Musical Meter.* New York: Oxford University Press.

Lutz, C. & White, G. (1986) The anthropology of emotion. *Annual Review of Anthropology*, 15: 405–436.

Lynch, M.P. & Eilers, R.E. (1991) Children's perception of native and non-native musical scales. *Music Perception*, 9: 121–132.

MacDonald, R.A.R., Hargreaves, D.J. & Miell, D. (2002) *Musical Identities.* Oxford: Oxford University Press.

MacNeilage, P.F. & Davis, B.L. (2000) On the origin of internal structure of word forms. *Science*, 288: 527–531.

Manturszewska, M. (1990) A biographical study of the life-span development of professional musicians. *Psychology of Music*, 18: 112–139.

Maslow, A.H. (1976) *The Farther Reaches of Human Nature.* New York: Penguin Books.

Maslow, A.H. (1968) *Toward a Psychology of Being.* (2nd edition). New York: Van Nostrand Reinhold.

McClary, S. (1991) *Feminine Endings: Music, Gender and Sexuality.* Minneapolis, MN: University of Minnesota Press.

McPherson, G.E. (2005) From child to musician: skill development during the beginning stages of learning an instrument. *Psychology of Music*, 33: 5–35.

McPherson, G.E. (Ed.) (2006) *The Child as Musician: A Handbook of Musical Development.* Oxford: Oxford University Press.

Merriam, A.P. (1964) *The Anthropology of Music.* Evanston, IL: Northwestern University Press.

Mesquita, B. & Frijda, N.H. (1992) Cultural variations in emotions: a review. *Psychological Bulletin*, 112(2): 179–204.

Meyer, L.B. (1956) *Emotion and Meaning in Music.* Chicago, IL: University of Chicago Press.

Meyer, L.B. (1967) *Music, the Arts, and Ideas. Patterns and Predictions in Twentieth Century Culture.* Chicago, IL: University of Chicago Press.

Miell, D., MacDonald, R. & Hargreaves, D. (Eds.) (2005) *Musical Communication.* Oxford: Oxford University Press.

Mithen, S. (1996) *The Prehistory of the Mind: The Cognitive Origins of Art, Religion, and Science.* London: Thames & Hudson.

Mithen, S. (2005) *The Singing Neanderthals: The Origins of Music, Language, Mind, and Body*. London: Weidenfeld and Nicholson.

Monson, I.T. (1996) *Saying Something: Jazz Improvisation and Interaction*. Chicago, IL: University of Chicago Press.

Neisser, U. (Ed.) (1982) *Memory Observed. Remembering in Natural Contexts*. San Francisco, CA: W.H. Freeman & Co., 414–417.

Nettl, B. (1983) *The Study of Ethnomusicology: Twenty-nine Issues and Concepts*. Urbana, IL: University of Illinois Press.

Nettl, B. & Russell, M. (Eds.) (1998) *In the Course of Performance. Studies in the World of Musical Improvisation*. Chicago, IL: University of Chicago Press.

North, A.C. & Hargreaves, D.J. (1997) Music and consumer behaviour. In D.J. Hargreaves & A.C. North (Eds.) *The Social Psychology of Music*. Oxford: Oxford University Press.

North, A.C. & Hargreaves, D.J. (2008) *The Social and Applied Psychology of Music*. Oxford: Oxford University Press.

North, A.C., Hargreaves, D.J. & Hargreaves, J.J. (2004) Uses of music in everyday life. *Music Perception*, 22(1): 41–77.

North, A.C., Hargreaves, D.J. & McKendrick, J. (1999) The influence of in-store music on wine selections. *Journal of Applied Psychology*, 84(2): 271–276.

Ockelford, A. (2007) *In the Key of Genius: The Extraordinary Life of Derek Paravicini*. London: Hutchinson.

Oldham, G.R., Cummings, A. Mischel, L.J., Schmidtke, J.M. & Zhou, J. (1995) Listen while you work? Quasi-experimental relations between personal–stereo headset use and employee work responses. *Journal of Applied Psychology*, 80(5): 547–564.

O'Neill, S.A. & Sloboda, J.A. (1997) The effects of failure on children's ability to perform a musical test. *Psychology of Music*, 25: 18–34.

Palmer, C. (1989) Mapping musical thought to musical performance. *Journal of Experimental Psychology: Human Perception and Performance*, 15: 331–346.

Palmer, C. & van de Sande, C. (1993) Units of knowledge in music performance. *Journal of Experimental Psychology: Learning, Memory and Cognition*, 19: 457–470.

Papousek, H. (1996) Musicality in infant research: biological and cultural origins of early musicality. In I. Deliège & J. Sloboda (Eds.) *Musical Beginnings. Origins and Development of Musical Competence*. Oxford: Oxford University Press, 37–55.

Papousek, M. (1996) Intuitive parenting: a hidden source of musical stimulation in infancy. In I. Deliège & J. Sloboda (Eds.) *Musical Beginnings. Origins and Development of Musical Competence*. Oxford: Oxford University Press, 88–112.

Park, C.W. & Young, S.M. (1986) Consumer response to television commercials: the impact of involvement and background music on brand attitude formation. *Journal of Marketing Research*, 23: 11–24.

Parncutt, R. (2006) Prenatal development. In G.E. McPherson (Ed.) *The Child as Musician: A Handbook of Musical Development.* Oxford: Oxford University Press, 1–31.

Parncutt, R., Sloboda, J.A., Clarke, E.F., Raekallio, M. & Desain, P. (1997) An ergonomic model of keyboard fingering for melodic fragments. *Music Perception*, 14: 341–382.

Patel, A. (2007) *Language, Music and Brain.* New York: Oxford University Press.

Pavlicevic, M. (1997) *Music Therapy in Context: Music, Meaning and Relationship.* London: Jessica Kingsley.

Pavlicevic, M. & Ansdell, G. (Eds.) (2004) *Community Music Therapy.* London: Jessica Kingsley.

Peretz, I. & Zatorre, R.J. (Eds.) (2003) *The Cognitive Neuroscience of Music.* Oxford: Oxford University Press.

Pickles, V. (2003) Music and the third age. *Psychology of Music*, 31: 415–223.

Pinker, S. (1997) *How the Mind Works.* London: Penguin.

Pitts, S.E. (2000) *A Century of Change in Music Education.* Aldershot: Ashgate Press.

Pitts, S.E. (2005a) *Valuing Musical Participation.* Aldershot: Ashgate Press.

Pitts, S.E. (2005b) What makes an audience? Investigating the roles and experiences of listeners at a chamber music festival. *Music and Letters*, 86: 257–269.

Pitts, S.E. (2007) *Anything Goes*: a case study of extra-curricular musical participation in an English secondary school. *Music Education Research*, 9: 145–165.

Pitts, S.E., Davidson, J.W. & McPherson, G.E. (2000) Developing effective practice strategies: case studies of three young instrumentalists. *Music Education Research*, 2: 45–56.

Pouthas, V. (1996) The development of the perception of time and temporal regulation of action in infants and children. In I. Deliège & J. Sloboda (Eds.) *Musical Beginnings. Origins and Development of Musical Competence.* Oxford: Oxford University Press, 115–141.

Povel, D.J. (1981) Internal representation of simple temporal patterns. *Journal of Experimental Psychology: Human Perception and Performance*, 7: 3–18.

Povel, D.J. & Essens, P.J. (1985) Perception of temporal patterns. *Music Perception*, 2(4): 411–440.

Pressing, J. (1988) Improvisation: methods and models. In J.A. Sloboda (Ed.) *Generative Processes in Music. The Psychology of Performance, Improvisation, and Composition.* Oxford: Clarendon Press, 129–178.

Prickett, C. (1998) Music and the special challenges of aging: a new frontier. *International Journal of Music Education*, 31: 25–36.

Rainbow, B. & Cox, G. (2006) *Music in Educational Thought and Practice.* Woodbridge: Boydell Press.

Rauscher, F.H., Shaw, G.L. & Ky, K.N. (1993) Music and spatial task performance. *Nature*, 365: 611.

Rauscher, F.H., Shaw, G.L., Levine, L.J., Wright, E.L., Dennis, W.R. & Newcomb, R.L. (1997) Music training causes long term enhancement of preschool children's spatial-temporal reasoning. *Neurological Research*, 19: 2–8.

Reynolds, R. (2002) *Form and Method: Composing Music (The Rothschild Lectures)*. S. McAdams (Ed.) New York and London: Routledge.

Rice, T. (1994) *May It Fill Your Soul: Experiencing Bulgarian Music*. Chicago, IL: University of Chicago Press.

Robson, C. (2002) *Real World Research* (2nd edition). Oxford: Blackwell Publications.

Rouget, G. (1985) *Music and Trance: A Theory of the Relations between Music and Possession*. Chicago, IL: University of Chicago Press.

Sacks, O. (2007) *Musicophilia: Tales of Music and the Brain*. London: Picador.

Sawyer, K. (Ed.) (1997) *Creativity in Performance*. Greenwich, CT: Ablex Publishing Corporation.

Seashore, C.E. (1938/1967) *Psychology of Music*. New York: Dover Books.

Shaffer, L.H. (1981) Performances of Chopin, Bach and Bartók: studies in motor programming. *Cognitive Psychology*, 13: 327–376.

Shove, P. & Repp, B. (1995) Musical motion and performance: theoretical and empirical perspectives. In J. Rink (Ed.) *The Practice of Performance. Studies in Musical Interpretation*. Cambridge: Cambridge University Press, 55–83.

Sloboda, J.A. (1982) Experimental studies of music reading: a review. *Music Perception*, 2: 222–236.

Sloboda, J.A. (1985) *The Musical Mind. The Cognitive Psychology of Music*. Oxford: Oxford University Press.

Sloboda, J. A. (1986) Cognition and real music: the psychology of music comes of age. *Psychologica Belgica*, 26: 199–219.

Sloboda, J.A. (1991) Music structure and emotional response: some empirical findings. *Psychology of Music*, 19: 110–120.

Sloboda, J.A. (1992) Psychological structures in music: core research 1980–1990. In J. Paynter, T. Howell, R. Orton & P. Seymour (Eds.) *Companion to Contemporary Musical Thought*. London: Routledge, 803–839.

Sloboda, J.A. (2005) *Exploring the Musical Mind: Cognition, Emotion, Ability, Function*. Oxford: Oxford University Press.

Sloboda, J.A., Davidson, J.W. & Howe, M.J.A. (1994) Is everyone musical? *The Psychologist*, 7: 349–354.

Sloboda, J.A., O'Neill, S. & Ivaldi, A. (2001) Functions of music in everyday life: an exploratory study using the Experience Sampling Method. *Musicae Scientiae*, 52: 9–32.

Sloboda, J.A., Parncutt, R., Clarke, E.F. & Raekallio, M. (1998) Determinants of finger choice in piano sight-reading. *Journal of Experimental Psychology: Human Perception and Performance*, 24: 185–203.

Small, C. (1998) *Musicking: The Meanings of Performing and Listening*. Hanover, NH: University Press of New England.

Smith, J.A. (Ed.) (2003) *Qualitative Psychology: A Practical Guide to Methods.* London: Sage.

Snyder, B. (2000) *Music and Memory: An Introduction.* Cambridge, MA: MIT Press.

Standley, J.M. (1998) Pre and perinatal growth and development: implications of music benefits for premature infants. *International Journal of Music Education,* 31: 1–13.

Stebbins, R. (1992) *Amateurs, Professionals, and Serious Leisure.* Montreal: McGill-Queen's University Press.

Stebbins, R. (1996) *The Barbershop Singer: Inside the Social World of a Musical Hobby.* Toronto: University of Toronto Press.

Sternberg, R. (Ed.) (1999) *Handbook of Creativity.* Cambridge: Cambridge University Press.

Stock, J.P.J. (2004a) Documenting the musical event: observation, participation, representation. In E.F. Clarke & N. Cook (Eds.) *Empirical Musicology.* Oxford: Oxford University Press, 15–34.

Stock, J.P.J. (2004b) Ordering performance, leading people: structuring an English folk music session. *World of Music,* 46: 41–70.

Stratton, V.N. & Zalanowski, A.H. (2003) Daily music listening habits in college students: related moods and activities. *Psychology and Education: An Interdisciplinary Journal,* 40(1): 1–11.

Strunk, O. & Treitler, L. (Eds.) (1998) *Source Readings in Music History.* New York: Norton.

Suda, M., Morimoto, K., Obata, A., Koizumi, H. and Maki, A. (2008) Cortical responses to Mozart's sonata enhance spatial-reasoning ability. *Neurological Research,* 30(9), 885–8.

Sudnow, D. (2001) *Ways of the Hand. A Re-Written Account.* Cambridge, MA: MIT Press.

Sundberg, J. (1988) Computer synthesis of music performance. In J. Sloboda (Ed.) *Generative Processes in Music.* Oxford: Clarendon Press, 52–69.

Sundberg, J. & Verillo, V. (1980) On the anatomy of the retard: a study of timing in music. *Journal of the Acoustical Society of America,* 91: 772–779.

Swanwick, K. (2001) Musical developmental theories revisited. *Music Education Research,* 3(2): 227–242.

Swanwick, K. & Tillman, J. (1986) The sequence of musical development: a study of children's composition. *British Journal of Music Education,* 3: 305–339.

Tagg, P. & Clarida, B. (2003) *Ten Little Title Tunes: Towards a Musicology of the Mass Media.* New York: Mass Media Music Scholars' Press.

Talbot, M. (Ed.) (2000) *The Musical Work: Reality or Invention.* Liverpool: Liverpool University Press.

Tarrant, M., North, A.C. & Hargreaves, D.J. (2002) Youth identity and music. In R. MacDonald, D.J. Hargreaves & D. Miell (Eds.) *Musical Identities.* Oxford: Oxford University Press, 134–150.

Temperley, D. (2001) *The Cognition of Basic Musical Structures*. Cambridge, MA: MIT Press.

Thayer, R.E., Newman, J.R. & McClain, T.M. (1994) Self-regulation of mood: strategies for changing a bad mood, raising energy, and reducing tension. *Journal of Personality and Social Psychology*, 67(5): 910–925.

Todd, N.P. (1985) A model of expressive timing in tonal music. *Music Perception*, 3: 33–58.

Todd, N.P. (1999) Motion in music: a neurobiological perspective. *Music Perception*, 17: 115–126.

Tolbert, E. (2001) Music and meaning: an evolutionary story. *Psychology of Music*, 29: 84–94.

Trainor, L.J. & Trehub, S.E. (1992) A comparison of infants' and adults' sensitivity to Western musical structure. *Journal of Experimental Psychology: Human Perception and Performance*, 18: 394–402.

Trehub, S.E. (2006) Infants as musical connoisseurs. In G.E. McPherson (Ed.) *The Child as Musician: A Handbook of Musical Development*. Oxford: Oxford University Press, 33–49.

Trehub, S.E. & Trainor, L.J. (1998) Singing to infants: lullabies and playsongs. *Advances in Infancy Research*, 12: 43–77.

Trehub, S.E., Unyk, A.M., Kamenetsky, S.B., Hill, D.S., Trainor, L.J., Henderson, J.L. et al. (1997) Mothers' and fathers' singing to infants. *Developmental Psychology*, 33: 500–507.

Trevarthen, C. (1999–2000) Musicality and the intrinsic motive pulse: evidence from human psychobiology and infant communication. *Musicae Scientiae*, Special Issue on Rhythm, Musical Narrative, and Origins of Musical Communication: 155–211.

Trevarthen, C. (2002) Origins of musical identity: evidence from infancy for musical social awareness. In R. MacDonald, D.J. Hargreaves & D. Miell (Eds.) *Musical Identities*. Oxford: Oxford University Press, 21–38.

Valentine, E. (2002) The fear of performance. In J. Rink (Ed.) *Musical Performance. A Guide to Understanding*. Cambridge: Cambridge University Press, 168–182.

Wallace, W.T. (1994) Memory for music: effect of melody on recall of text. *Journal of Experimental Psychology: Learning, Memory and Cognition*, 20(6): 1471–1485.

Wallin, N.L., Merker, B. & Brown, S. (Eds.) (2000) *The Origins of Music*. Cambridge, MA: MIT Press.

Waters, A.J., Townsend, E. & Underwood, G. (1998) Expertise in musical sight reading: a study of pianists. *British Journal of Psychology*, 89: 123–149.

Wiering, F. (2006) Comment on Huron and Veltman: Does a cognitive approach to mode make sense? *Empirical Musicology Review*, 1(1): 56–60. Available at: https://kb.osu.edu/dspace/bitstream/1811/24073/1/EMR000004b-wiering.pdf (accessed 25 August 2009).

Williamon, A. (2002) Memorising music. In J. Rink (Ed.) *Musical Performance. A Guide to Understanding*. Cambridge: Cambridge University Press, 113–126.

Wilson, G. (1997) Performance anxiety. In D. Hargreaves & A. North (Eds.) *The Social Psychology of Music*. Oxford: Oxford University Press, 229–245.

Windsor, W.L. (2000) Through and around the acousmatic: the interpretation of electroacoustic sounds. In S. Emmerson (Ed.) *Music, Electronic Media and Culture*. London: Ashgate Press, 7–35.

Wood, D. (1988) *How Children Think and Learn*. Oxford: Blackwell.

Yalch, R.F. (1991) Memory in a jingle jungle: music as a mnemonic device in communicating advertising slogans. *Journal of Applied Psychology*, 76(2): 268–275.

Zatorre, R.J. & Peretz, I. (2005) Brain organization for music processing. *Annual Review of Psychology*, 56: 89–114.

Zillmann, D. & Gan, S. (1997) Musical taste in adolescence. In D.J. Hargreaves & A.C. North (Eds.) *The Social Psychology of Music*. Oxford: Oxford University Press, 161–187.

Index